Food journalist and podcaster **Gilly Smith** was an early adopter in British food podcasting, and was nominated for a Fortnum and Mason award in 2017 for the *delicious.* podcast. She is the producer and presenter of *Cooking the Books with Gilly Smith*, the *delicious.* podcast, Leon's *How to Eat to Save the Planet*, *The Borough Market Podcast* and *The Write Songs*. She produces The Food Foundation's *Right2Food* podcast and Philip Lymbery's *The Big Table* podcast for Compassion in World Farming.

Initially a radio and TV producer, she has written seventeen books, mainly about the influence of culture of food in its various forms, as well as articles for the national press and academic journals, largely about food, philosophy and ethical travel. Smith's *Taste and the TV Chef* (2020) won the UK Gourmand Award for Food Writing.

How to Start and Grow a Successful Podcast

Tips, Techniques and True Stories
from Podcasting Pioneers

••••••••••••••••••••

Gilly Smith

A How To book

ROBINSON

ROBINSON

First published in Great Britain in 2021
by Robinson

10 9 8 7 6 5 4 3 2 1

A CIP catalogue record for this book
is available from the British Library.

ISBN: 978-1-47214-534-5

Typeset in Sentinel and Scala Sans
by Ian Hughes

Printed and bound in Great Britain by Clays
Ltd, Elcograf S.p.A.

Papers used by Robinson are from well-
managed forests and other responsible
sources.

MIX
Paper from
responsible sources
FSC® C104740

Robinson
An imprint of
Little, Brown Book Group
Carmelite House
50 Victoria Embankment
London EC4Y 0DZ

An Hachette UK Company
www.hachette.co.uk

www.littlebrown.co.uk

How To Books are published by
Robinson, an imprint of Little, Brown
Book Group. We welcome proposals
from authors who have first-hand
experience of their subjects. Please set
out the aims of your book, its target
market and its suggested contents in an
email to howto@littlebrown.co.uk.

For Jed, Elly and Loulou

Contents

Foreword

Not many things in life can prepare you for discovering that your father has been secretly writing pornography in the garden shed. And when this singularly nightmarish event happened to me, I can guarantee that reading it aloud on a podcast was the last thought to enter my mind. So how did I come from abject horror to nearly 300 million downloads? What was it about broadcasting smut with two mates from my kitchen table that caught the world's imagination? And perhaps most bizarrely, why doesn't my dad know *anything* about sex?

An emergency pub session with my best mates was the beginning of its journey. I knew that suppressing this bile would be more unhealthy than confronting it head on, so with my friends' encouragement I began reading a few lines of *Belinda Blinked* aloud. Inevitably those few sentences became a few chapters, a few glasses of wine became a few bottles and before we knew it, we had quite literally emptied this posh north London boozer of all clientele. *Belinda Blinked* was addictive, outrageous, gold.

I had long been making things together with two of the friends in attendance, James and Alice, stretching back to our time in the student television society at the University of Leeds (geek alert!) so we immediately recognised the potential of *Belinda Blinked*. We knew we wanted to do something with it. The question was what. The material was too salacious for a web series, too risky for a broadcaster. But self-produced audio seemed the perfect fit. Much like how the *50 Shades* phenomenon benefited from the anonymity of ebooks, we figured people could 'enjoy' Belinda's adventures in the privacy of their own headphones.

What's more, *Serial* had just debuted in the US and all three of us had become obsessed with Sarah Koenig's forensic investigative journalism. This would be somewhat . . . different, but it was clear podcasting was back and we were ready to give it a go.

None of us had ever tried our hand at podcasting before, but buoyed by the excitement of sharing Dad's x-rated world we threw our hats into the ring. We loved the idea of being able to fully control our own show with nothing off limits. Having worked for years in traditional media, with endless rounds of notes and approvals, we suddenly felt the sense of liberation we'd been craving since those halcyon university days. It really felt like anything was possible and the rules were there to be written. There were so few blockbuster podcasts that the conventions of the medium were yet to be established, and in so many ways they still are.

Creating podcasts is as much about the boldness of your approach as the execution of your ideas so a show really can be whatever you want it to be, regardless of precedent. The learning curve may be steep, but with no expectations comes nothing to lose. Did we think anyone would be interested in a sixty-year-old's ill-judged fantasies? We had no idea. Was it worth exploring if they would? Absolutely.

The democratisation of media has long been the barrier to boundary-pushing content, but with podcasting anyone can tell a story they're passionate about with minimal expense and technical knowledge. A traditional broadcaster would never have commissioned *My Dad Wrote a Porno*, but they don't need to. All that's required is a good idea, strong work ethic and the confidence that your show can find an audience. And in many instances they do. It's one of the very few meritocracies of storytelling left, where a little show like ours can stand shoulder to shoulder with the big guns of NPR and the BBC. Not because of brand recognition or marketing budgets, but because the podcast itself struck a chord with listeners. There's nothing more exhilarating or rewarding than making your own show and knowing it found success on its own merits.

Our little show was born from the humblest of beginnings and we've ridden a wave beyond any of our expectations. And in many ways we benefited from there being no precedent for it. In 2015, when we started, it was still very much the podcasting Wild West with a whole new world to discover and opportunities to be mined. There were very few 'live episodes', never mind full-blown world tours which eventually saw us sell out venues like the Royal Albert Hall and the Sydney Opera House four times over. Podcasting hadn't gone 'mainstream' yet so the thought of three Brits having their own show on HBO in the States was laughably inconceivable.

We just made a podcast. No expectations, no pressure.

We set out with one singular mission – to make a great show that we ourselves would want to listen to. If people tuned in, then great. If not, we'd still have fun reading this atrociously delicious book together. And as we're about to embark on series six, we're still just three mates huddled around a kitchen table, microphones balancing precariously on cookbooks, making each other laugh.

There's a simplicity to podcasting that is so captivating and addictive, not only to the listener but to the creator too. The liberty you have to make your own show on your own terms has been the most creatively freeing experience of my career. Plus I've been able to share it all with my two best mates and my mad, miraculous dad. I highly recommend giving it a go; it's blinking brilliant.

Jamie Morton, co-creator, My Dad Wrote a Porno

To get access to *How to Grow a Pod,* the accompanying podcast series that includes full interviews with podcasting pioneers and other exclusive material, scan the QR code below:

Introduction

Peta and Adam are professional pet sitters. Ten years ago they traded their flat for a nomadic adventure that has taken them across the world, cuddling dogs and soothing their owners' brows as they settle into palatial properties and cosy cottages to pamper pets for a living. They have a story to tell and the voices for podcasting. They've even got a name: *Sit; Stay: adventures in nomadic pet sitting*. But where do they start? Would anyone be interested in their podcast? How would anyone find out about it? What's the focus? What kit do they need? What investment is required? How long does it take?

The average podcaster uploads between three and five episodes before giving up. The average adventurer doesn't get around to making one. This book is for people like Peta and Adam. But it's also a brief history of podcasting for freelancers, small-business owners, big-business owners and people with something to say to an audience that increasingly wants to listen. With how-to advice from some of the most successful podcasters in Britain, this is the definitive guide to telling your own stories and getting heard.

I've been podcasting since 2016 when I was first handed the keys to the *delicious.* podcast, the British food magazine *delicious.'* nascent foray into audio storytelling and interviews. The goal was to add a layer of sound to the brand's light mix of delightful cooks, food writers and celebrity chefs and to the human stories behind the food we eat. Although it was an early adopter in the glossy magazine world and among the first British food magazine podcasts, it came late in the day to the wider podcasting world, particularly in America. I've watched the scene change from an amateur playground with freelance journalists and have-a-go hobbyists making it up as they go along to a fertile hunting ground where producers and sponsors sniff out the best new talent and grow them into podcasting celebrities. As the shape-shifting finds ever new forms, podcasters burrow into their niches: the big money pods, the communities of practice, the rambles with your mates, the audio portfolio, the sound of the business. Podcasting is a great big melting pot, a DIY world in which anyone of any colour, creed or character has a place on the stage.

Showing you how to get your voice heard among the millions of others on that vast multinational stage is the job of this book. With more than 1,500,000 shows, 34 million episodes (according to iTunes in October 2020) in more than one hundred languages in 155 countries, podcasting is growing exponentially, and we are but drops in its vast ocean. Around 7.1 million people in the UK now listen to podcasts each week, an astonishing one in eight people and an increase of 24 per cent over the past year, according to Ofcom. Its research found that half of listeners have joined the podcast wave in the last two years. In this book, you'll learn how to surf it.

In conversation with the early adopters and the late developers, we learn from their mistakes and how to get it right. From the bedrooms and garages where some of our favourite podcasts first began, to the studios and boardrooms where podcasts have become a serious marketing must-have, this is the first book to take the freelancer, storyteller, small- or big-business owner or blogger through the how and *why* of podcasting.

What makes a podcaster?

The podcast that makes the number one slot is the Holy Grail, the pearl in the oyster, the four-leafed clover. It's the goal, something that releases you from the day job, that makes you enough money and gives you enough credibility to take Fridays off. It's what every podcaster wants. Isn't it?

Well . . . Not always. Maybe you like your day job but you want somewhere fun to play with your toys. Maybe you want someone *else* to play with your toys with you. Perhaps you want to play with your toys while a whole load of people who also like your toys listen to you. Throw in a little envy from your listeners and you may well have your pearl. Welcome, you're a podcaster.

Maybe you're not really driven by making money but you quite fancy the idea of taking Fridays off. Life-work balance is your goal, and you want to build a community, have some fun and learn something new. Sounds to me like you're self-employed, running your own business or working freelance, choosing your own terms over the payroll, lower stress levels over company ambitions. You're used to making it up as you go along. You're like me, an adventurer, an entrepreneur, a lateral thinker, a ducker, a diver, a podcaster.

Maybe you're on the payroll but you're bursting with ideas that your boss just doesn't understand. You're a communicator, a storyteller, a networker and you've got an idea that will use the best of your talents to get the company message out into the world. You love listening to podcasts. You've got a voice and something to say. You're a podcaster in search of a podcast. Come on in.

Or maybe you just want to change the world.

I've met you all in the online forums and the meet-ups, my one-day podcasting courses for the National Council for the Training of Journalists and my podcasting retreats at my home in East Sussex. The foodies who can't wait to get home to bake for Instagram; the self-employed consultants who want to share what they know in so much more than a blog; the communications teams who have been given carte blanche by their trusting boss to have a go at podcasting; the poets, artists, comedians, writers, musicians, activists who are fed up with the commissioning process, the curation by white men in suits, the time it takes to be greenlit. They all come my way with little more than a notebook, an app full of their favourite shows and questions they don't even know how to ask.

Some want to hear how I learned to podcast and some want to know how I made it my day job. Some want to know how within six months my first, the *delicious.* podcast, reached number one in the UK food charts, knocking BBC Radio 4's flagship *Food Programme* off the top spot on several occasions, and how it came to be nominated for the coveted Fortnum and Mason award in the Radio or Podcast category before it was even a year old. Most want to know if it makes money.

Some want to know how to find a subject that no one else is podcasting about, how to get consistently great guests, travel the world and have the kind of life that Instagram dreams are made of. Others are suitably sceptical and want the real story. How long does it take? How many downloads does it take to get to number one in the UK food charts? Is that even a thing compared to the US food charts? Who cares about the charts in this strange new podcasting world? Most ask about the money.

So, here's my story. I was teaching multimedia broadcast journalism at the University of Brighton in 2016 when I was approached by my would-be boss at *delicious.* magazine to take over their brand new podcast. Although I'd been teaching podcasting as part of the course, I'd never actually made a podcast. I was interviewing him using a broadcast quality iPhone microphone (Zoom iQ7 MS Stereo Microphone for iOS), and when he asked me if I could edit, I told him that I'd been editing in one form or another all my professional life. Like the pioneers in podcasting you'll meet in this book and on its accompanying podcast *How to Grow a Pod,* I've worked in the media since I left university, learning how stories work, how to shape them and how to edit them into something someone else would want to hear, read or watch. I began my career in radio and, like many of my interviewees here, I too think 'tape' when I'm recording or editing after years of physically cutting audio tape, captured on a reel-to-reel (Uher) and spliced with a razor blade. Such editing devices have long since been replaced by endless examples of computer software, but the imagery and legacy of reel to reel, razor blade and splicing tape live on. I was in.

The budget for the *delicious.* podcast was tiny, nowhere near enough to pay for my decades of experience or the mortgage, but the marketing and editorial team and I were in it together. We all knew that we were donning our cowboy hats and heading into the Wild West, making it up as we went along and if it made money, we'd all be winners. My mission: to take *delicious.* readers by the hand into Nigella's sitting room, Yotam Ottolenghi's kitchen, out to lunch with Rick Stein, to ask questions on their behalf, to introduce the younger podcast listening community to the *delicious.* brand and gently lead those who hadn't a clue what a podcast was into a whole new world of stories in sound.

Like most freelance journalists, I'm a portfolio worker with a number of storytelling strings to my bow and as the internet offers ever new platforms on which to tell mine, I scrub up my skills. Repackaging stories was something I'd taught my multimedia journalism students and I had no idea then that a story would have so many homes as it does now. These days, it's smart to find the core of a story and look where it can reach, monetising, leveraging and gathering followers all along the way; from experts in their fields to adventurers in life, a story can have as many outlets as there are people interested in the story. It's also a good idea to have a second income ...

You'll find some of those stories here: *My Dad Wrote a Porno,* the tale of three friends from university who turned the hilarious moment when one of their dads shared his erotic hobby with his son into a podcast, a book, a world tour and a small fortune; *The Missing Cryptoqueen,* born of a BBC producer's obsession with a mysterious tech story that no one seemed to have spotted, who then turned it into an award-winning podcast series and sold it to the highest bidder to make into a feature film; the young black poet who gave up rapping to become a podcaster and change the world.

We find what success in podcasting looks like. The *delicious.* podcast was never going to make me my fortune, but over the four years I told its stories, it was like doing a PhD in food which has a value way beyond its tenure. I had permission to learn everything there was to know about the relationship between food, farming and climate change (my pet subject). It was a fascinating challenge to deliver it to a mainstream food-lover from the comfort of a big-name magazine brand and with the support of its team. I was fed a constant diet of the latest food books, trends and products, taken around the world by publicists and brands to fast-track my knowledge on everything from the wines of California and Bordeaux to the food of north-east Thailand and the fifty best restaurants in the world. I was given a pass to interview the biggest names in the business, to develop relationships with them and their publicists, filling a little black book to die for and building an ever firmer base for my career in food podcasting. Without a studio, I was free to go wherever the story was and to capture the sounds and feel in a way that had previously been the remit of the skilled wordsmiths at the magazine. It was a dream of a job, but I relied on my retreats business to pay the mortgage.

Although I had worked in food for twenty-five years by then – from radio food reviews to TV food politics and writing books about food culture – the *delicious.* podcast gave me the exposure, the authority and the voice to leverage me into a new position in the food community. As a mature woman returning to a full-time career after focusing on my children first and food journalism second, it propelled me into an exciting and glamorous world I thought I'd forfeited years before as a stay-at-home mum with a part-time university career. The inclusive, ageless, meritocratic culture of podcasting and the social media world of food is not, sadly, reflected in the Ambition Commission, the phrase coined by George the Poet to describe the powers that threaten to stymie this plucky, punky do-it-your-own-way world of storytelling. Its advertisers and broadcasters are still obsessed with the idea that millennials prefer to listen to people their own age; that aspiration will always be towards youth and beauty.

No change there. But podcasting has other fish to fry. It has opened the door to anyone who has something to say. With excellent microphones and voice recording apps as standard on most smartphones, a podcast is accessible to anyone. It is colour, age and sex blind, and in 99 per cent of cases it's only as successful as its listenership decides. With no commissioners, no bosses to say, 'No you can't', the podcast has outstripped the blog as the most democratic platform in the media landscape.

In this book, we'll meet some of the podcast pioneers who have made it up as they've gone along, creating new templates in storytelling and debunking myths about how to get your voice heard. We'll find out what they use to record on and edit with, how they tell their stories, find their listeners and build a community who love what they do. We'll learn from their mistakes and stock up on their tips. We'll peek behind the smoke and mirrors to find out how to make the podcast of your dreams and, if you want to, how to make your millions.

So what do you want to say? Who do you want to speak to? What do you stand for in the world? If podcasting really is that easy, that accessible, what are you going to do with it? Over the course of this book, I hope you won't just find out how but *why* to podcast. Armed with the tools to get your message out into the world, you'll discover how to drill down into what that really is with the people who have found their fans and made an impact on people's lives.

PART I:

The Basics

1

How Did We Get Here?

Once upon a time in Podcastland, there were some plucky pioneers. We'll meet many of them here in this book, chuckling at their luck and timing, and generously sharing their stories from the front line. They came from the world of entertainment – drama, news, music – but they wanted to do it their own way. Blogging had carved a new stream out of the rocky, unwieldy world of broadcast and print media, and as the waters came alive with vibrant new voices, the hobbyist wild swimmers turned the tide and changed the world.

Journalist Nicholas Quah has been charting its history and packages it (already) in terms of eras. From the 'First Era' of the mid-2000s, the pioneers were making it up as they went along with audio versions of blogs a natural progression of the democratic use of the internet. When the *Guardian*'s Ben Hammersley coined the term 'podcast', no doubt borrowed from Steve Jobs' 2001 iPod, to pad out an article on this new movement, a phenomenon was given form.

When in 2005 Apple began to build a directory of podcasts on its iTunes music store, later adding a podcast app as standard to its iPhones, finding and subscribing to podcasts became effortless, and a new industry began to emerge as fans found communities in this new media space. But around 2009, as the internet filled with new music and video streaming services, the appetite for DIY audio storytelling waned. Sound and story fans remained loyal to the glorious examples created by *This American Life* and *Radiolab*, which stayed at the top of the iTunes charts, but by 2014 podcast listening figures had evened off. Until, that is, the creators of *This American Life* blasted podcasting into the media stratosphere with *Serial* and, for Nicholas Quah, into the second of his eras, 'The Boom Years'. According to Edison Research, which has led the podcasting stats since 2006, the number of monthly podcast listeners in America more than doubled in the five years after *Serial*'s launch in 2014, from around 39 million Americans to an estimated 90 million. In the five years preceding 2014, the same metric grew by only 35 per cent.

By 2017 the arrival of *S-Town*, again by the *This American Life* team, reached 40 million listeners in just three months and advertisers formed a boisterous queue. A study by the Interactive Advertising Bureau in 2019 found that podcast revenue grew from $314 million in 2017 to $479 million in 2019. Quah predicts that advertising revenue could hit $1 billion by 2021.

The game was changing, and quickly. Quah called what's happening now the third era, 'Big Podcasting': when Spotify bought Gimlet Media (*Heavyweight*, Esther Perel) and Joe Rogan and when Luminary persuaded everyone's favourite podcaster, Russell Brand, to wrap himself in gold behind a paywall. It's the era of colonisation when BBC Sounds brings its preferred suppliers, the indie production companies that make the lion's share of BBC radio programmes to the party, and Hollywood hands its 'maybe' piles of scripts to its new podcast producers as an inexpensive way to try them out on an audience. For many podcasters, it's a spending spree in which they're the product.

But it's not just how many people are listening to podcasts that is making the marketeers prick up their ears: it's who they are, and more interestingly how much they might be spending. MusicOomph.com found that, according to studies by Edison and Neilsen, in the US at least podcast listeners are young, educated and have money to spend. Forty-five per cent of podcast listeners have an annual income of a quarter-of-a-million dollars, and they're extremely well-educated; 68 per cent are more likely to be postgraduates. Female podcast listeners appear to have higher education and income than the overall US population. It's a trend that British brands are watching with interest.

Podcasting has settled itself into the place that books used to occupy, teaching, entertaining and compelling listeners who no longer like to read. It's mostly an immersive, solitary experience, enjoyed with a host of new friends in your head through the magic of noise-cancelling headphones, but an eight-part true crime podcast can just as easily keep a family or a couple entranced for hours on a road trip or an evening around the fire, a nostalgic echo of the listening experience around the old radiogram of the 1930s. 'I think that people just love podcasts for their ability to learn something new,' says Josh Adley, director of communications at London production company Listen. 'You might listen to true crime because you get into the story, you might listen to a history podcast because you want to learn something or you might listen to that celebrity conversation because you're really fascinated by what they have to say. There's such variety and it's just so accessible. I think that's what's changed over the past few years. People have started to see that there are really well-produced podcasts out there that are worthy of their time.'

In the UK, Ipsos Mori reported its findings from a 2020 survey with MIDAS, RAJAR's audio survey. It reported an increase of 45 per cent in the previous year to 9.4 million podcast listeners in the UK. Combining its data with the BBC's, it found that Londoners show the highest levels of usage, with 23 per cent of respondents listening every week, probably driven by longer commuting journeys. Thirty per cent of podcast listeners listen when driving or travelling, and 18 per cent when relaxing. Fifty-nine per cent of podcast listeners listen to the entire audio episode, and 62 per cent listen to all or most of the episodes they download. Eighty-nine per cent of podcast sessions are a solo activity. Like the American audience, podcast fans are likely to be 'from higher social grades'; according to Ipsos Mori, 12 per cent of ABC1s (the 'highest earning and best educated' adults) listen every week compared to just 5 per cent of C2DEs at the other end of the demographic scale.

And that's a very interesting trend to watch for all podcasters, whether or not you intend to monetise. Over the course of this book and its accompanying podcast, *How to Grow a Pod,* we'll find out why. You'll hear from the podcasters who have made millions and those who have made no money at all. There are those whose work has broken new ground and inspired new forms of storytelling, and those who have found thousands of new friends to share their passion. Along the way, you'll find out how and why to make a podcast, get tips from the people who made it work, and advice from those who'll tell you not to bother. But perhaps most of all, you'll feel the spirit of podcasting rising in your veins.

2

Really Saying Something

If podcasting is the democratic dream of a platform, the space where everyone has the right to speak, this is your opportunity to say what you really feel, to express a part of yourself that hasn't had a chance to be heard before. So, before we start with the basics of how to make a podcast, let's pause a moment. *What* do you want to say and *who* do you want to say it to?

It's the thrill of telling a story that has people signing into podcast support groups, joining classes or messaging podcasters to ask which microphone to buy. But few who I meet at my retreats or classes have really drilled down what it is that they're going to use it for. 'I want to make a podcast about my life.' 'I want to chat about stuff with my mates.' 'My business partner and I rap really well about everyday work stuff. That might be funny for someone.' These are all real answers and real possibilities. But they need some excavation.

There are many reasons for making a podcast in the twenty-first century: for many people it's a hobby but for others it's a business card, the blog *de nos jours*. It can be a powerful addition to your marketing toolkit, and if you get it right, it can make your work life more fun and more successful; or it can be something that simply makes you and your listeners happy. Whatever the reason, finding its purpose can bring the clarity you need for your content.

Sometimes, it's just the moment when opportunity and nous collide, as you'll read in many of the stories from the podcast pioneers peppered through this book. For some, it's the 'I can do that' moment that drove Jessie Ware to create her award-winning *Table Manners* podcast with her mother, Lennie; for others, like the *My Dad Wrote a Porno* team, it's the *kerching* sound of podcast gold landing in your lap. For Olly Mann, who admits he always wanted to be a broadcaster, it was the combination of spotting the moment, the chutzpah of youth and the sensibility of a young media producer that made him one of the most successful podcasters in the UK with *Answer Me This!!*, *The Week Unwrapped* and *The Modern Mann*.

For businesses and organisations, a podcast can offer a creative tool to tell the stories most people never hear; the Church of England's *The Good Stuff* and *Generous June* podcasts come from the communications team at the Diocese of Winchester and, despite being scuppered by lockdown in June 2020, they continued to spread the word of the Lord when the chips were down.

Award-winning podcast producer and playwright Chris Hogg used the unlikely format of a drum 'n' bass musical to tell the story of eating disorders to a young audience in his podcast *Cassie and Corey*, while award-winning audio storyteller Hana Walker-Brown joined a podcasting team at Broccoli (p. 186) which created an equality pact that would change the industry. Its inventive and utterly compelling podcasts are the public sound of its commitment to diversity and equal rights.

Marketing queen Susie Moore, in her course *Five Minutes to Famous* (fiveminutestofamous.com), says that anyone can find their voice through a little self-examination. She suggests asking some serious questions of yourself to find out who you are in the world of stories:

- Who do I represent?
- What do I stand for?
- What conversations do I want to start?
- What conversations do I want to be part of?

In the crowded world of social media, these questions are the Marie Kondo of podcasting. If the answers don't spark joy, delete, breathe, repeat the process until the hairs on the back of your neck stand up. Anything less is clutter. Bouncing ideas off someone else is often the quickest way to sort your identity wardrobe. Instead of asking yourself, ask a friend. Who do I represent? What do I stand for? In short, who am I? You may be surprised at the results.

Jane is a marketing consultant who likes to get out and meet people. She wanted to make a business podcast but didn't know how to frame it and so came to me for a one-on-one session. I asked her what she loves best about her job. Every week she meets interesting people and listens to their stories, filing them away in her encyclopaedic brain. She gives her clients what they need in terms of business advice and gets to know them really well. She described herself as 'a great networker', but prodding a little at what that means revealed a rare skill. Jane is a super-listener. People want to sit next to Jane at business dinners because she *really* hears what they have to say. And, as if she's making a giant social jigsaw, she will spot the missing piece. 'You need to meet x,' she'll say, pulling a memory from the reservoir of her vast social network. And she delivers. Jane won't just take a business card after her chat; she'll follow up with a connecting email. I asked her what she writes in that email. 'Something like "Let me introduce . . .",' she told me. And there it was, the meat – and the title – of her podcast. Jane's podcast is an introduction to the people she meets through her business, a fascinating insight into the ordinary people in her business through the extraordinary lens of Jane's super-listener skills. For a niche business community like Jane's, that's podcast gold.

Food writer Miranda Gore Browne was a finalist on the first series of *The Great British Bake Off* and finds most of her work as an authority in baking as a public speaker, demonstrator or writer. In the crowded world of cookery, her success is driven by her prolific online presence and she is keen to find new ways to generate fresh and interesting material on all platforms. Like many self-employed writers, she has to be clear about who she is in a cluttered social media landscape and to differentiate herself from the other British bakers in the field. Her Instagram Live videos are fun – and she managed to entertain her three children throughout lockdown by co-opting them onto her 'shows' as mini-bakers, immediately propelling herself into the pared-down community of bakers-with-kids-who-cook.

But what Miranda needed when she came to my Guild of Food Writers' retreat was to find out what made her unique. As her fellow food writers and I workshopped what her podcast could be, we quickly noticed that Miranda loves a natter, and not just about *anything* either. She's a warm, empathetic person who people feel drawn to, and as she pours a cup of tea and cuts a slice of cake, it's almost impossible to fight the urge to open up. People tell her their secrets, hopes and fears as effortlessly as she whips her batter, and life appears to lighten. It's as if she's mixed a truth-telling potion into the buttercream. She told us how, for her, cake is a catalyst and how much of her writing is inspired by the conversations she has over an Elizabeth sponge. 'It's more than cake,' she told us. We looked at each other with a knowing nod. 'What?' she asked, looking at our smiling faces. *More than Cake* is now Miranda Gore Browne's occasional podcast featuring teatime chats and bite-sized confessionals.

Podcast pioneer: George the Poet

Some people just want to change the world. George Mpanga, aka George the Poet, knew why he wanted to make a podcast even before podcasting was a thing. At the invitation of his religious studies teacher, twelve-year-old George wrote how he would like to be remembered at his funeral: as 'an entertainer with influential views', he wrote, the words appearing on the page before he knew they had even formed in his mind. 'Children just know things, man,' he tells us in his award-winning podcast *Have You Heard George's Podcast?* 'I'm the proof. There's a certain clarity that comes from youth. Because deep down, young people just want the truth.'

'I was a rapper from fifteen to nineteen, and I transitioned into poetry for very practical reasons, actually,' he said. Grime, the style of rap that he was using, was very fast. 'If you weren't used to listening to it and encountering me for the first time you might not catch everything I said,' he told me. 'And I thought the practical way around this is to take the same lyrics that I would perform as a grime MC and speak them conversationally. And that made a lot of sense. That took me to the entertainment space.'

George is a poet with purpose. He was born and grew up in Neasden, north-east London, with his three brothers, two sisters and his parents who had emigrated from Uganda. His paternal grandmother is the Ugandan politician and former cabinet minister Joyce Mpanga, and George's mother was the force behind his acceptance into the elite grammar school, Queen Elizabeth's in Barnet, a thirty-mile train journey every day from his home and his friends. It was here that George recognised that education meant opportunity. Just five weeks after graduating from Cambridge University, the young rapper was signed to Island Records. 'I was most driven to write by the stories inside me,' he told me. 'There is a popular representation of those stories that can miss the nuance that I find most fascinating. I was constantly working on how to capture nuance and complexity and the social milieu that create the impression of the 'hood, the inner city.'

The learning curve at Island Records was, he said, like a Masters degree. 'That's when I saw the early application of my poetry scaled up almost as a crash course. no one had a clear plan of how to do it, but there were some wins. I realised the value of PR. I realised the value of fame and what it can achieve.' His period at Island Records would eventually lead to his epiphany in podcasting, the pioneering make-it-up spirit that was the essence of his style of rap poetry: 'Grime didn't have the interest or the investment, respect or protection of any of the big players in music or audio at the time,' he said. 'So that led to a very DIY culture and that helped us immensely.'

But business is business and it was the measure of success in terms of metrics that would lead him to rethink how best to use his voice. 'There were a lot of losers in that space,' he told me. '*I* felt like a loser in that space. To use it as a parallel example of innovation to podcasting, it was an exciting space. There was a variety of voices – quirky, sombre, stern, pained, fun-loving but there was always a bias towards what the majority of the audience wanted to hear. And my work didn't fare well under that bias. I stepped away from that space because it was very unlikely that our interpretation of success would align.'

Big actors began to get involved with this cool young talent: TV, corporates, Radio 4. 'People wanted to pay me to present intelligently, to do what I really wanted to do without having the metrics that were so important in grime. I didn't have the biggest following. I was just stubborn, hard to place but what I wanted to do was very clear. I wanted to do poetry.'

George had been working on the sustainability agenda with the United Nations' publicity machine, Project Everyone, which was promoting sustainability development goals (SDGs) as an accessible framework for change. 'Up to that point, my poetry had been a little bit scattergun,' he told me. 'I'd do a little on unemployment, I'd do a bit on climate change, water shortage, grain shortage, cancer research, and it was all important work. But I wanted to know that I was moving forward in a systematic way. I felt like I was cross-pollinating different storytelling technologies.'

It was a podcast about inspiring leaders in business and social movements called *How I Built This* that would give George his storytelling eureka moment. He noticed that the podcast episodes were mostly an hour long, but found himself short-changed by a half-hour episode on Richard Branson. 'That's when a lot of the storytelling questions converged on the form of podcasting,' he said. 'I realised that people expect a continuation and because of the model they've chosen they expect to listen for an hour.' In an hour, he realised, he could begin to tell the stories that matter to him. 'It would give me the space to elaborate the nuance that I don't think I was great at mastering in pop music.'

Used to the three-minute pop song to deliver his message, suddenly the elasticity of time in podcasting gave him the space to play. 'Not to take anything away from popular music,' he added. 'Some people are great at bringing out nuance in that form, but having written so many essays for so long at an intense level, I was used to the deep dive.'

It became clear that podcasting was the perfect platform for his art form.

Have You Heard George's Podcast? is a question not just about the way he tells his stories from the streets, framing them within his unlikely education and subsequent opportunities and delivering them back to the people he so wants to hear them, but the art form he and his producer, the classical composer and pop music producer Benbrick, play with. 'He saw me on Jools Holland just as I was finishing my degree at Cambridge,' George told me when I asked how the meeting of minds happened. 'We batted about a few musical ideas but he was the same as me; he felt the form that had been handed to him by the industry by our expectations as consumers just wasn't it. There was something else. So he started experimenting with film music.'

What we had never heard before could only happen on a podcast. With nothing but a 'suitcase full of sound effects and instruments' and an explosion of ideas, he and Benbrick created the podcast in George's spare room, releasing the first season in 2018.

George deliberately played with our minds. He could conjure up images from inside his head and transmit them directly into ours. And without a budget in sight.

George messed with our cultural signifiers, the stuff we'd all grown up with, regardless of circumstance. It was the cartoons (he quotes *Hotel Transylvania, Finding Nemo, Despicable Me*) that George would watch with his young nephews which inspired the sound and feel of the podcast. 'I fell in love with the boundlessness of the animation,' he told me. 'The representation of physical bodies is literally elastic. But the music is taken very seriously in children's entertainment.' He connected it to the film music he grew up with – *Beauty and the Beast, Aladdin, The Lion King* – and realised that it was some of the best music he had heard in his life. He wanted to create an experience that necessitated the use of film music. Listening to Disney on his phone was life-changing. 'Music amplifies and intensifies the experience and there it was,' he said. 'I thought, *Imagine if I could create intentional messaging.*'

George uses the signposting technique that the founder of *This American Life,* Ira Glass, employs so well, the rupture of the narrative that calls the listener to action. Close your eyes. Come back. Did you hear what happened there? 'First of all, I wrote to the score of *American Beauty,*' George told me. 'I grew up as a rapper and we used film or instrumental music as a blank canvas. I would close my eyes and listen to *Beauty and the Beast, Pocahontas, American Beauty, Desperate Housewives*, the Danny Elfman *Batman* work and I would triangulate my way to my current truth – and I would challenge myself to find my truth that I was experiencing today – and in trying to construct that in the mind of the listener, I became quite literal. I just told myself, you're going to have to ask them to close their eyes and you're going to make *that* part of the entertainment.'

I asked him how long it was before he felt that he'd done it, that he had felt heard. 'I think it's quite telling that I came up with the title before writing a single line of it,' he laughed. 'It was a confluence of a lot of questions I've had for a long time. The podcast was the answer. When you feel that alignment within yourself, it is your job to make it apparent to everyone else.'

By 2019, the podcast was nominated in six different categories at the British Podcast Awards: Best Current Affairs, Moment of the Year, Best Arts & Culture, Best Fiction, Best New Podcast, and Smartest Podcast, winning the last four plus Podcast of the Year. BBC Sounds was quick to commission a second season later that year, plucking George from independent podcaster to part of the Corporation. 'No path to becoming a public voice is straightforward,' he said when I asked him why he had accepted the BBC deal. 'There are pros and cons to every pathway and I feel I've done every pathway.'

His friends had been concerned about the comparatively low listenership of his first series of *Have You Heard* and had urged him to think about a machine that could promote him and provide the funds to do what he really wanted to do. But he had faith. 'I'd finally found my form,' he told me, referring to the first award-winning season of the podcast. 'My job was perfecting the form. I had faith in people to recognise what we'd done here. I felt what we needed to do would become clear.' Scaling up was becoming necessary; they needed the money. 'Charging the audience would have killed it for me,' George said. 'I wanted it to be free. I wanted a partner whose focus wasn't commercial.' He wanted to work with an organisation that had an understanding of the commercial landscape, which had commercial ambitions but could fulfil his purpose to 'link the streets with the intelligentsia'. It had to be the basis of the relationship with the partner who was going to present his passion to the world. He found it in BBC Sounds who reached out to him and offered him the world. 'They didn't change a single thing,' he told me. 'They haven't interrupted the flow.'

Does he think that his childhood premonition has come true? Is he making an impact as an entertainer? 'It's never been clearer,' he said. 'People understand the complexities that took me a long time to understand about myself. When they hear it, they understand it in themselves, so now we're having a much more sophisticated conversation than what we had before.'

<<<You can hear the whole interview with George the Poet on How to Grow a Pod.*>>>*

TECH talk

George uses an Aston Spirit microphone. 'They're a young company that have transformed the microphone space. I find their mics affordable, high quality and versatile. They can capture a range of tones very well.

'We record the podcast using Logic. Benbrick has like a room full of suitcases of sound effects, instruments that will allow us to create very quickly some quite elaborate scenarios. And that's pretty much it, man. The bare mechanics are pretty easy and the rest is up to you and how hard you push yourself.'

POD POINTS

Find out what you want to say by asking yourself:

- Who do I represent?
- What do I stand for?
- What conversations do I want to start?
- What conversations do I want to be part of?

3

Planning Your Podcast

Your granny was right: failing to plan is planning to fail. In this chapter, we look at the building blocks that make sure all the grand plans you've honed over the last couple of chapters – what your show is about, why you're doing it and who you want to listen – see the light of day.

Any embryonic idea has to find form, and writing a clear proposal will aid a safe birth. One of the good things about our automated age is that where once a kindly chap might have leafed through your etchings, poems or first draft of a novel, these days most ideas have to be submitted in a form. From title to a sixty-word summary to a list of bullet points for the marketing team, everything must be drilled down from a vague idea to a well thought-through plan if it's to be taken seriously. And this may well make the difference between your bedroom fantasies and the podcast of your dreams.

A podcast host – the automated system which turns your mp3 into a podcast, assigns it an RSS code and catapults it into the world – will take you through the same process as you upload your work for the first time with prompts for maximising impact. (By the way, RSS? You don't need to know, but it stands for Really Simple Syndication and is the web feed that allows users and applications to access updates to websites in a standardised, computer-readable format. It's okay, it's automated by your host. You never need to ask again.)

But we're getting ahead of ourselves. Let's answer the key questions: What's unique about your idea? Why you? Tell me in very few words why I should listen. You'll be paying your podcast host on a monthly basis pretty soon, so save yourself some money and plan your pod now.

The title

We've discussed the importance of a title in Chapter 2 in terms of digging deep into what you want to say, but in an ocean of podcasts, you'll need a title to grab your listener; to make them laugh, if that's what you want them to do; to tell them to listen up, if that's what it's about for you. Do your research. Have a look at the podcast page on your iTunes app (go to 'store' and select 'podcast' on the drop-down menu) or scroll through your podcast app, noticing which ones you chose because of the title alone. The chances are that you subscribed through word of mouth, but if you didn't, was the title memorable enough to remember? I'm listening to *The Teacher's Pet* at the moment, a suggestion given by friends during a discussion of the best true crime series for a road trip. I traded *The Missing Cryptoqueen* and *Fake Heiress* for *The Teacher's Pet* and a couple of others whose names I don't remember. The story of an Australian football star and PE teacher whose affair with his sixteen-year-old student led to the disappearance of his wife in the eighties sounded like just the binge listen I needed for the long drive ahead on our weekend away. *The Teacher's Pet.* I could see it. What are the odds it makes it to Netflix? I'm three episodes in and I haven't even packed yet.

It was a no-brainer to call Borough Market's podcast *The Borough Market Podcast* and *delicious.* magazine's podcast the *delicious.* podcast, yet when I took the latter over after only four episodes, it was called *dish.* Unfortunately, this is also the name of the *Sunday Times* food magazine. It had to go, and as we were only just off the starting blocks, we changed the logo and the title and no one really noticed. It would have been a different story if we hadn't spotted the error quite so quickly.

Happily, a title can be changed easily enough in the settings of your podcast host and the altered RSS information will be reflected in iTunes automatically. When I chose *Cooking the Books* as the title for my latest food books podcast, I thought I could get away with the fact that there was another podcast with the same title because it was hosted by a New Zealand chef – until I started to list it manually with all the other directories. I found that there were at least four other podcasts around the world with the same title. I popped into the settings on my podcast host, Acast Open, and within seconds I had changed it to *Cooking the Books with Gilly Smith*. Acast sorted the rest automatically.

With Leon's *How to Eat to Save the Planet*, it was trickier. The brief from the restaurant chain was to create a six-part series about sustainable food as part of their new *Leon Presents* platform whose big claim was to make its listeners and YouTube viewers 'better humans'. The various documentaries, shows and podcasts produced for the platform were created to help us all do our bit for climate change and become healthier and happier along the way. As we whittled down the subject areas for my Leon food podcast, we agreed that most people want to know more about if or how they should eat meat, dairy and fish, save waste and understand veganism. They wanted to eat out *and* in but without a heavy carbon bill. But what to call it? Words like sustainable, climate, carbon or waste just didn't fit with the cool call to action that Leon wanted. It was my daughter who asked me what it was actually about. 'How to eat to save the planet,' I told her. 'Well, that's what it's called then,' she said. Sometimes the title is right under your nose.

The subtitle can give more information. *Cooking the Books with Gilly Smith: Where food is the story* gives you an idea of what you're going to be hearing, but subtitles don't make it to the logo. Keep it in your plan, if only to remind yourself what it's about.

The logo

Like a good title, an arresting logo can make all the difference in an overcrowded marketplace. If you haven't got a celebrity name attached to your podcast, all you're aiming to do at this stage is to grab attention. Once your listeners have subscribed, each episode will pop into the feed on their podcast app automatically, but if they don't and they're trying to remember your title to tell their mates, a quick search through their recent listens on their podcast app could find it. Unless, that is, your logo looks like all the others.

Business podcasts may want to reflect their brand in their logo and require the use of a graphic designer, but for most hobbyists it's a fun challenge although it may incur a cost. I spent £75 on a freelance designer to work on the *Cooking the Books* logo and shared her drafts with my Facebook community who voted on their favourites. My brief was the title and subtitle, *Cooking the Books: Where food is the story*. I told her that it was about food in books and books about food, that it was for people who liked food and books. I wanted my name on it, it had to follow the podcasting guidelines of being clearly visible when shrunk to a tiny thumbnail and it needed to be delivered as a 1400px x 1400px to 3000px x 3000px square jpeg. Apple Podcasts require artwork to be delivered at a 72 dpi resolution JPEG or PNG format using RGB colour space. Beyond that, I left it to her.

Among the several food- and book-based images, there was one that grabbed me (and most of my Facebook friends): three silicone spoons laid head to toe in lime, red and teal with 'Cooking', 'The' and 'Books' in the scoop of each. Against a black background, the teal 'Gilly Smith' and red 'where food is the story' stood out. Sadly, a podcasting expert pointed out that when shrunk down to thumbnail size, it would be pretty but impossible to read. The final choice was a zooming in of that original image with the whole title on the middle spoon and just a hint of the lime and teal spoons still in view, 'Gilly Smith' in black dynamo font against the lime and 'where food is the story' on the teal.

Does it matter that the new title isn't reflected in the logo? no one has mentioned it...

When UK podcasting matriarch Helen Zaltzman stimulated a discussion about logos among members of her Facebook Podcasters' Support Group, the thread was fascinating. Suzy Buttress posted her logo for her *Casual Birder* podcast, a simple drawing of a bullfinch on a perch. 'I wanted something that simply conveyed birds and birdwatching,' she wrote. 'A friend helped convert a photo of a bullfinch from my garden, I had it made into a drawing and he added the binocular outer aspect, which really sets it off. I love it! And I have had people tell me it is one they related to.' Suzy was among several respondents to the thread who posted the original photograph.

Wil Treasure's *Factor Two* podcast, produced in conjunction with UKClimbing.com, has a striking black-and-white logo of a climber on a postage stamp. 'I silhouetted a photo I took a few years ago and I wanted it to have a "stamped" look, for no reason other than I liked it,' he wrote, posting the original photo too. 'I was quite pleased to manage to incorporate a piece of climbing equipment into the text.'

Zachary Tyler King-Turner posted a simple black-on-yellow lettered graphic for his *After Dark: True Crime, Conspiracy Theories* podcast. 'I really wanted to go with the black and yellow colour scheme,' he wrote. 'The yellow really pops and the glow kinda ties it together. The backing art is a picture my partner/co-host took, which really helped tie everything together! It's simple, but I like how it turned out!' Krister Greer posted his pink and yellow *Now That's What I Call Music!-*inspired logo for his podcast *Pop: Collaborate and Listen*. 'We're about nineties music,' he wrote, 'so [I] wanted a nineties feel to it, and we wanted it to look a bit like the "Now" albums so a friend came up with this.' 'Love it!' replied a podcaster in the group. 'And you've just done an episode about The Cure's "Wish" so consider me subscribed!' Clearly the logo works.

Among our podcasting pioneers, whose stories are captured

in these chapters and the accompanying podcast, are some winning images. The logo for *My Dad Wrote a Porno*, a rich red book emblazoned with the title in embossed gold lettering, captures a theatrical and regal feel for Rocky Flintstone's erotic novel, despite the team having no idea at the time of launch of how multi-platform the podcast would become. The image for *Table Manners with Jessie Ware* neatly sums up the relationship between clear-headed, slightly grumpy Jessie and her wine-loving mum Lennie as they sit at the dinner table, waiting for their guest. George the Poet stands stern and purposeful against a black and red background for his podcast logo, while the *Anthems: Pride* series, in which daily essays inspired by one word cracked open a door into the world of LGBTQAI life for thirty days in the run-up to Pride 2020, uses a simple rainbow.

The summary

This is what Chris Hogg calls 'the sip pitch'. While some call it 'the elevator pitch', Chris points out that no one really pitches anyone in a lift, whereas plenty of partygoers get the opportunity to answer the question, 'What's your podcast about?' while their interrogator and potential listener takes a sip of their drink. Chris answers, 'It's a drum 'n' bass comedy musical about eating disorders.' no one walks away after that.

Have a browse through your favourite podcasts' summaries. Our podcast pioneers have nailed it:

- *Table Manners*: 'Jessie Ware hosts a podcast about food, family, and the beautiful art of having a chat, direct from her very own dinner table. With a little bit of help from her chef extraordinaire mum Lennie, each week guests from the worlds of music, culture and politics drop by for a bite and a bit of a natter. Oversharing guaranteed.'

- *The Log Books:* 'Stories from Britain's LGBT+ history and conversations about being queer today.'
- *The Missing Cryptoqueen:* 'Dr Ruja Ignatova persuaded millions to join her financial revolution. Then she disappeared. Why? Jamie Bartlett presents a story of greed, deceit and herd madness.'
- *Have You Heard George's Podcast?:* 'The award-winning and critically-acclaimed podcast from George the Poet delivers a fresh take on inner city life through a mix of storytelling, music and fiction.'
- *The Old Songs Podcast:* '*The Old Songs Podcast* explores the stories behind traditional songs – where they came from, who sang them, how they've changed and where they're going.'
- And mine? '*Cooking the Books* is for people who love to read about food. Season 1 is about food which explores plot, motivation and characterisation, while Season 2 features all your favourite food writers from Gill Meller, Olia Hercules and William Sitwell among many, many more. Gilly Smith (the *delicious.* podcast, Leon's *How to Eat to Save the Planet*) finds what's cooking in the minds of our literary stars.'
- Leon's *How to Eat to Save the Planet:* 'Food journalist Gilly Smith looks at how we make the way we eat more environmentally sustainable by rolling back the years to a time when food came from around the corner, when living off the land meant living lightly on the planet – and to find out how to do it now.'
- The *delicious.* podcast: 'The chart-topping podcast for the UK's best food magazine, *delicious.* magazine, featuring stories and hot topics from the world of food. From small producers to the best chefs in the world, from delightful dishes to the big issues in health, food waste and sustainability, from high-profile interviews to words of wisdom from the country's most

thoughtful food writers, the *delicious.* podcast explores just about everything that's on the plate in 21st century Britain.'

So, what's yours?

The summary form won't prod you to think any more deeply when you upload your podcast, but while you're planning, it's useful to imagine how you would sell it. What makes it unique? What will people learn? What does it achieve? List five points, if only to sharpen your marketing tools. You'll need them later.

The market

Who is your target audience? Before you start to think about your social media campaign, considering your target audience is crucial. Where and who is your community? If you're a hobbyist (*Star Trek*, birding, folk songs . . .) where do other fans hang out? How can you reach them?

For me, it's all about food, from food writers and chefs to campaigners and producers. I hope that my Facebook and Instagram (less so, Twitter, but only as a personal preference) reflects my hobbyist enthusiasm and my journalistic integrity and knowledge. Remember Susie Moore's advice in Chapter 2 and it will ensure you keep the stories coming and project a vibrant and authentic voice on social media. Who do I represent? I represent food lovers who care about where food comes from and its stories, about animal welfare and its connection with saving the planet, about taking time to appreciate the culture and politics of food. What do I stand for? I stand for integrity, creativity, imagination, solutions, community, energy. What conversations do I want to start? How can we change the way we eat to save the planet? What conversations do I want to be part of? How we can change the way we eat to save the planet.

Podcasters' plans

I asked the vibrant community of online podcasters in Facebook's Podcasters' Support Group to give me their plans in six points. Tracey Casler of *Lady Jupiter Podcast* bullet-pointed hers:

1. Determine audience
2. Differentiate from blog of same name, podcast accompanies blog
3. Pick rundown – three sections that are easy to talk about
4. Use a script – only because I'm prone to ramble
5. Upload handful of episodes before launch – so listeners can jump right in and find me in all directories
6. Be as excited to edit as you are to record

Matt Rafferty of *The Author Inside You* podcast gave me his: '1. After our kids left for college, I convinced my wife to co-host a podcast with me where we interview new authors about writing, publishing, and promoting their book. Our intent is to motivate writers to publish that book they have always been dreaming about. 2. We find our guests by word of mouth and by reaching out to interesting authors and 3. we conduct most of our interviews via Facetime audio. 4. I edit with Final Cut Pro and 5. we host the show with Libsyn ($15/month). 6. As for social, we mainly use FB. Recently we have been creating a promotional video for each new episode.'

Each podcaster is different. We may read the host's newsletters (Buzzsprout's is particularly worth a subscribe) and share ideas in the forums but most of us will take the tips and do it our own way. My plan with each of my podcasts goes something like this:

1. Know what I want to say and who I want to say it to
2. Find the best guests that I can via the publicity machine or the campaign and go back through my own contacts

3.   Find the format that works for the podcast
4.   Prepare well and record to time. Time = money, so don't waste it
5.   Instagram pictures and stories of the process, from recording through to episode, to let the audience feel part of the adventure
6.   Release weekly and share everywhere. Make your Podcast Day a thing!

You're almost ready. You've got your title, its look and feel and you've wrapped it up in the words that will communicate what you want it to do. But what's in it? In the next chapters, we'll look at format, the narrative arc of your show and, if you're having guests, how to book them. As we head into storytelling, you'll almost be ready to buy your mic and start playing with editing software.

POD POINTS

- Failing to plan is planning to fail
- Who are you talking to and why?
- Express your answers clearly in your title, logo and summary
- What's your sip pitch?

4

Format and Ramble

With so much to say, how best to say it? You've come up with your 'Big Idea' and worked out a plan but if you're hoping that sitting across a kitchen table with a co-host is all you need to create a show like *Table Manners with Jessie Ware* or *My Dad Wrote a Porno*, think again. You can read the full story behind *My Dad Wrote a Porno* in Chapter 14 (p.133) and hear it on the podcast, but Alice Levine explained to me how they tried to make the idea of three best friends sitting around their kitchen table reading from a parent's erotic novel sound 'loose'. 'We didn't want it to be an hour-and-a-half of stream-of-consciousness,' she said. 'It's always followed the same format, and that's kind of a bit of chat, a bit of establishing our week, a bit of talking amongst ourselves, recapping where we're at and then diving into what is the heart of the podcast, which is the chapter.'

In the middle of every good rambling podcast, you'll find structure and direction. 'I was really obsessed with *The Trip* with Steve Coogan and Rob Brydon,' said Jessie Ware, who had been looking for an idea for a podcast before she landed on *Table Manners*, the cooking-with-guests show that she presents with her mother, Lennie. She wanted to make a podcast that was about something other than her music, more like a hobby. Something like *The Trip* seemed perfect. 'Well, they have a really nice time,' she told me. 'They go to a nice restaurant and chat.' She wondered if she could do something similar, eating out and having a conversation over dinner, but it was the prospect of dealing with too much atmospheric sound in a restaurant that had her thinking again. 'Mum's a really great cook and she's always hosted, so we thought that we could try and do it at my mum's house, and maybe that would be quite nice and cosy and disarming.' The original idea was still forming when Jessie invited her good friend, Radio 1 presenter Clara Amfo, to be their first guest. 'That episode is slightly different to the other ones,' she said, 'because we asked her which ingredients she liked so that we could cook something around that. But it felt too much like a MasterChef challenge. It was quite stressful for my mum and me to think, *What can we make out of chorizo and sweet potato?* And so we thought, *They'll get what they're given.*' As a former TV researcher and the daughter of a *Panorama* journalist, Jessie knows how to construct a story: 'So there was that format: you're coming to my mum's house or mine for dinner and we're going to talk about food.'

But it wasn't *just* about food, and this blasted open the show's appeal to an audience of millions. It was the opposite of niche; it was about *life*. 'It's about memory,' said Jessie. 'You look at something like *Desert Island Discs* which has such a beautiful arc, a beginning, middle and end – it's so simple. That's very satisfying. You are always going to have a unique conversation with somebody about food and memory. And that was the jackpot for this that I didn't realise that I was sitting on.'

A good format can be a golden ticket, particularly in broadcasting where it can be replicated in different languages with different hosts in territories all over the world. Think *MasterChef, Who Wants to be a Millionaire?* and *The X Factor*, where the rights of the originals have made the producers a fortune. It might be pushing it a little to imagine such a win in podcasting, although Ira Glass may disagree; *This American Life* has followed its famous format since 1995. But the shape of a show is an excellent way to build an audience; the listener knows what to expect, and if they like it, they'll come back for more. Hitting 'subscribe' to the podcasts you relate to will curate your own list of favourite listens in your podcast app, and in the vast plains of Podcastland it will help you navigate through to the streets where you belong.

Some formats are easier than others and for some businesses or media products its podcast may simply be its sound-sister. Producer and co-founder of the British Podcast Awards, Matt Hill, told me how in 2017 he started and grew the now hugely successful *The Week Unwrapped*, the current affairs podcast for *The Week* magazine presented by Olly Mann, which digests world news into what it considers to be the most important stories of that week. Matt was invited to distil the essence of the magazine into something new for the podcast. 'The point of the magazine is that they show you the best journalism from around the world,' he told me, 'and, depending on which country the magazine's in, particularly that country's journalism – so in this case the UK. The show was built around the idea that we could take three stories that were under-reported but have a massive impact for our lives. Every show three members of the news team from the TheWeek.co.uk would give you their best shot at what will be the story we'll be talking about in ten years' time. We change the names and the stories change, but actually the template is very similar week after week.'

A format can also be a handy way of connecting you with an audience that's already engaging with similar shows. 'Ours was the current affairs show that wasn't tackling the same stories as every other current affairs show,' said Matt. 'We quickly found a kind of current affairs junkie audience. If you listen to *Electioncast* or *Brexitcast*, this is the show you listen to next because you get a completely different list of stories. So, it's like you've got part two of the news after the break.'

Bringing podcasting pioneer Olly Mann on board to present the show meant that it started life with a massive audience. The full story of how Olly and Helen Zaltzman grew their first show, *Answer Me*

This!!, in 2007 to become one of the most successful British podcasts ever is recounted in Chapter 16 (p.154), but working with a magazine can have its downside. As with the *delicious.* podcast for *delicious.* magazine, it simply wasn't the main priority for the publisher of *The Week*, Dennis Publishing. 'It took them a long time to tell their audience about it,' said Matt. 'They were a bit nervous, and the magazine and the digital side didn't always communicate with the other, so it took a while to even get an advert in the magazine.'

Being in the right place at the right time is a stroke of luck for most podcasters, but for professionals like Matt and Olly, they were there more often than not and, as they talked about the show, influential people began to hear about it. 'We got the ear of a couple of great podcasters who just really loved the show,' Matt told me. Pandora Sykes and Dolly Alderton present *The High Low*, another top current affairs podcast supplemented by a witty dusting of beauty chat and celebrity gossip, but they are also part of the millennial media scene; Sykes writes for *Elle* and the *Sunday Times* while Alderton is a columnist for *Sunday Times Style* magazine, and is now a feted writer. 'Pandora would often namecheck us for a story that she'd heard about that week, and mention *The Week Unwrapped*, and then suddenly we got this bump of *The High Low* audience coming to *The Week Unwrapped*, and then they'd stick around and then the audience churns around.'

Cross-pollination of podcasters – or 'cross promos' as it's known on the forums – can bring new audiences to podcasts big and small. Members of Helen Zaltzman's Facebook Podcasters' Support Group, for example, are invited every few months to briefly describe their podcast in a kind of subject-specific speed-dating game. 'Traditionally, the way of doing that was just to invite podcasters onto your show,' said Matt. 'But, I think, more importantly it's podcasters listening to your show and telling their audiences about it.' How to share a show if it doesn't have a celebrity presenter can often be down to its one-line tag. The simple format of BBC Radio 4's *Desert Island Discs*, in which the guest chooses eight songs, a book and a luxury to take to their desert island, has been endlessly reworked. The *Desert Island Dishes* podcast follows this format with the food its guest couldn't do without, and I've used it to inspire *The Write Songs* (on Mixcloud), in which my guests choose the five songs that 'wrote' their books. *Cooking the Books*, in which my guests choose four food moments from their latest book, is another iteration. As we use the songs and the moments to explore specific parts of their books, we learn much more about the process of writing, the experience behind the story and the feelings the writer has about it. In short, it gives a chat a focus and, for the listener, a sense of where the show is going and what to expect.

Yet despite the easy access a format will lend a show, podcasts have made rambling into an art form. *The Football Ramble* is a hugely popular podcast and has given the green light to anyone with something to say about, well, anything really to launch their own podcast. As a result, the podwaves are full of them: *Imaginary Rambles, Insane Rambles, Random Ramblings, Rambles of a Music Teacher, Rambling Stoners, Ramblings of an Undisciplined Mind,* even *AfroBrit Ramblings* – there's a podcast for anyone who fancies an hour or so with a random new friend.

The best rambles will be based around a list of bullet points shared between hosts in advance, which make all the difference to the flow of your episode. James Ramsden and his friend and business partner Sam Herlihy were early adopters of podcasting in 2014 with their rambling chat in *The Kitchen is on Fire* podcast featuring anything they had to say that week. They had been listening since 2013 to podcasts like *Harmontown* and *SModcast* with Kevin Smith, 'very white American dudes rabbiting on about nonsense,' said James, and it seemed easy enough to try it out themselves. 'I thought, well, we can rabbit on about nonsense quite well. Or at least, we thought we could.'

It resulted in what James bashfully calls a 'cult' podcast, although he admits that this is probably 'a bit of a euphemism', its listeners more committed than plentiful. 'We have never been tactical or had any strategy to growing our community,' James told me. 'We just like sitting down talking rubbish to each other and, in a rather solipsistic way, we thought let's record it and see who enjoys it.'

Keeping on keeping on is one of the most important mantras of a successful podcast, and James and Sam's two hundred-plus episodes are evidence that staying power works. The show has a listenership which James thinks is made up of those who knew them from his early supper clubs and food writing, and which has evolved over the years to include those who have loved their two restaurants, the award-winning Pidgin in East London and its now closed Mayfair sister, Magpie. It's added a new dimension to the community they inadvertently built. 'When we started, we didn't have the restaurants,' said James. 'Now industry people listen, but then our audience was probably made up of people who followed me or Sam or both of us on Twitter.'

They may have had a brand behind them, but it was *their* brand, packed with their own flavour, that gave the podcast its authenticity. It was deliberately ramshackle; they decided to use 'a list of notes' rather than a skeleton script to structure their hour-long show, and although Sam is a musician and technically articulate, they threw out the idea of an edit: 'We wanted people to feel like they were listening in rather than to an interview,' said James. 'We tried to be a bit more professional and, I guess, journalistic, but it quickly became clear that what worked best for us, if not the listeners, was to just have a chat.'

But even within their hour-long banter, there is something of a format which first pushed the show onto iTunes' New and Noteworthy category, the mark of a newly successful podcast after notable spikes in listening. 'It wasn't until we started getting regular guests that we started to see our numbers going up considerably,' said James. Their guests are usually fairly high profile in the food world, although, unlike me, the hosts don't expect them to share their episode. James told me: 'Some guests will be sweet enough to do an

Instagram story. It really does make all the difference.' And in the middle of their banter was the bit that many of their listeners were waiting for: 'We've always done games,' James told me. 'Back in the day when we were real rookies, we played cryptic games about restaurant dishes. I remember getting Susan Ray who's a BBC Radio 4 announcer doing intros to our games like the Joey Tribbiani recipe conundrum.' The game proved to be a useful device for some of their less confident guests. 'If they're not so jokey as we are, we say suddenly, "Right, you're going to play *Overrated, Underrated, Correctly Rated*," or the quickfire where we'll just say a dish and the guest has to give their gut reaction. Sometimes Sam will throw the games in quite early on if he thinks they need warming up. We'd think, *God how are we going to get through an hour with this person?*'

James and Sam are full-time restaurateurs these days, and post-COVID the podcast is even less of a priority. 'We're not ambitious about the podcast,' James told me. 'We check in on our stats and we're interested in why an episode might do well, but it was five years into the podcast that we set up the Instagram account. That's the level!'

Arguably, if you're already planning to interview guests, you're on your way to nailing your format. But how do you get your dream guests, and in a moment of reflection, why? In the next chapter, we'll find out.

POD POINTS

- Leverage interest from influential people if you can
- Decide on a format
- If you prefer a ramble to a more regimented format, make notes and share them with your co-host ahead of time
- The best rambles have structure to them

5

Booking Guests

One of the joys of podcasting is the opportunity to meet your heroes. Niche hobbyists and their celebrity leaders will love you because you not only speak their language, but you speak to their people too. The authors, singers, poets, designers, activists you follow on Instagram need your support, and they're all there at the click of a mouse. Of my many podcasting mantras, one of my favourites is: 'Yes, you can.'

Remote recording

As I write this, the country is in lockdown. I'm looking out over my meadow at the butterflies feasting on my artichokes and wondering what would encourage me to travel anywhere again. Remote interviewing hasn't just kept me working throughout this extraordinary pause in history, but it has opened doors into the homes of many people I might never have had access to. As a passionate advocate for reducing our carbon footprint to save the planet, working at home ticks my box.

It wasn't always thus. I didn't do remote. I wanted my interviews with my heroes to be up close and personal. I suggested – and usually got – lunch cooked by my food writer guests as a way of getting even deeper into their foodie psyches. I didn't even have to sneak a peek at their bookshelves; I could pick the most interesting titles off the shelf and discuss them in the flesh. For someone like me who has worked in food for my entire professional life, being in the company of the people who drive its bus, shift its gears and encourage new generations of thought leaders and food enthusiasts to get on board is a sheer joy. So, when I read *Hungry* by Jeff Gordinier, the former *New York Times* journalist and US *Esquire*'s food editor, in which he takes us on a one-off rock 'n' roll road trip with René Redzepi, one of the world's leading chefs, I desperately wanted him on *Cooking the Books*. He's one of the old-school food writers, a Tom Wolfe in Bourdain's clothing, but even if I had flashed my press card at the right people and had an article commissioned in return for a flight to New York, I've given up flying. He was, quite simply, off my list.

Enter COVID-19.

It was days after lockdown began in the UK that I had a meeting booked at BBC's New Broadcasting House with the *My Dad Wrote a Porno* team, Alice Levine, James Cooper and Jamie Morton, something I'd set up with their agent and which had taken months to organise. Liaising between busy media people is a challenge. I wasn't going to let it go. If I couldn't get there myself, I knew a few thousand podcasters who would have some suggestions. I checked into the Podcasters' Support Group on Facebook, searched 'remote interviews' and found a flood of responses to the dilemma.

- We use StreamYard. It records all video and audio on its own. You can use it without streaming, just click 'record only'. Plus, I record with Audacity as a backup. My co-host is in NY, and I am in VA.
- I really like Squadcast.fm.
- We tried Cleanfeed once, and the connection was so bad we didn't even record and went back to Zoom.
  Zoom's been mostly good considering the traffic, but last week we had a couple of issues.
- I've been really impressed with Zencastr.
- I use Zoom in a double-ender setup and with Zoom original sound recording as backup.

I live in the middle of the countryside and find Skype and Zoom freeze my face and echo my words as they try desperately to find enough signal on the country breeze. I need a clean feed, something that can't be distorted by the instability of my wifi. Julian Mayers at Yada Yada Productions was working remotely on a series for Audible and offered me a failsafe method which is so easy and works so well that I can't believe it is not used as a default technique. He told me, 'Record over Skype or Zoom but record your side on a good recorder' (I use Zoom H4N) 'and get them to record their side on something similar – like a smartphone using a recording app like Voice Memos and email you their audio. That way you can mix the two sides together in the edit.'

It's known as a double-ender, and it has set me free. With Zoom for the eye contact and headphones in our computers to avoid recording the other side's tinny Zoom voices, the *My Dad Wrote a Porno* team could join me from their own homes, each recording on their own professional recorders and emailing me a clean feed for the edit. I did the same. I even managed a peek at their bookshelves.

I emailed Jeff Gordinier, 'We're on.' As we effortlessly chatted, him in the Hudson Valley and me overlooking my meadow, I realised that this could go anywhere. I could take my listeners on a virtual summer holiday with me to Venice, home of food writer Skye McAlpine, to the Jurassic coast of Dorset where food writer Gill Meller was busy creating the vegetable garden of his Instagram followers' dreams, to Slovenia where Ana Ros, the best female chef of 2017 according to The World's 50 Best was locked down with her team of international chefs at her restaurant, Hisa Franco. Who else could I have on the show now that my needs were so much simpler? Who wouldn't do half an hour on Zoom for a bit of publicity? I tweeted one of my favourite authors, Joanne Harris, whose new book *The Strawberry Thief* was just out, the latest in the *Chocolat* series which I had devoured. 'Sure,' she said. 'Why not?'

The double-ender

All the interviews for the podcast accompanying this book as well as many for *Cooking the Books* were conducted using Julian's double-ender technique – sometimes a triple-ender as with Jessie and Lennie Ware, and in the case of the *My Dad Wrote a Porno* team a quad-ender. And it works a treat. On my hit list now are food writers from all over the world, people I could once only dream of interviewing and who will not only provide essential listening for anyone interested in food, but boost my knowledge, influence and audience. I even created a whole new podcast for The Food Foundation called *Right2Food* whose aim was to get behind the closed doors of lockdown life and capture the stories of some of the most vulnerable people in the country. Without being able to get to the charity's teenage food ambassadors myself, I taught them the superpower of turning their phones into microphones. The resulting podcast was ground-breaking. It was launched on Radio 4's *The Food Programme* in July 2020 and hugely increased awareness about child poverty in the UK. The material was used for background research and led to two documentaries on the work of The Food Foundation. The Marcus Rashford #endchildfoodpoverty campaign in September 2020 with FareShare, The Food Foundation and the big supermarkets used the audio in its social media tweets, and, perhaps most importantly, it gave people suffering from food poverty in the fifth richest country in the world an opportunity to tell their own stories, recorded on their own phones.

The promotional trail

So how do you get influential guests on to your show? The *My Dad Wrote a Porno* team tell us how Dame Emma Thompson and Elijah Wood asked *them* if they could appear on the show, while niche podcaster Jon Wilks bagged Billy Bragg *and* his fans for his *Old Songs,* but the spirit is the same for most podcasters: chutzpah. 'I bother them on Twitter or Instagram,' said James Ramsden of *The Kitchen is on*

Fire podcast. 'In almost all cases, I'll know them tangentially. Alex Andreou, who was on recently, we've followed each other on Twitter since I can remember being on Twitter.' James has 17,000 followers on Twitter and while his is a niche podcast, he was an early adopter and has built a dedicated audience. He and co-host Sam Herlihy are well known in the food community and fish for their guests in a fairly small pond. 'It's easy to say, "You're a food person; we're in the food business, we do a food podcast. Do you wanna be on?"' James told me that getting someone he was simply interested in talking to was harder. He told me about his pitch during the early days of the pandemic to an editor of a newspaper he followed on Twitter. 'He said, "Well, you're a food podcast, why do you want to talk to me?" I said, "We're in the middle of a global pandemic and you're editing a news website, so it would be interesting to have a chat."'

Jessie Ware told me that she ran out of A-list celebrity contacts from her 'little black book' by the end of Season 1. 'That didn't stop you!' said her mum, Lennie. 'She'd be doing *Jools Holland*,' she told me, 'meet someone she liked and say, "Do you want to come on our podcast?" And they would. And then it changed to people approaching us.' *Table Manners* quickly became a phenomenon, largely thanks to the winning juxtaposition of pop stars and music industry legends like Will Young, Sam Smith and Annie Mac at the Wares' kitchen table, and it is a fun invitation. But outside the green room, the have-a-go school of booking guests is alive and well. Maco Euan McAleece wrote on Facebook's Podcasters' Support Group how he managed to get an A-list actress on to a twenty-four-hour recording of charity comedy podcast *The CheapShow*: 'I watched the livestream of a charity comedy event happening in the theatre next to the studio I was working in. I waited until Gillian Anderson had finished her bit, then waited outside for her to come out. I politely ushered her into our studio. The PRs were furious. I cared not a jot.'

'The power of the ask is the most important thing in my view,'

Andy Wang of *Inspired Money* podcast wrote on Facebook's Podcast Movement Community. 'Invite thoughtfully and ask often. You never know who will say yes. Often yeses come back within twenty-four hours while others take far longer. Last year, I attended a LinkedIn event in New Jersey where I only knew one attendee. During the networking hour, I chatted briefly with one of the panellists, Maribel Lara, who is head of consulting at the Sasha Group (a VaynerX Company). In mentioning my podcast, Maribel suggested that I speak to her friend, Ramona Ortega, who had founded a FinTech company. I had Ramona on my show, and she was fantastic. I followed up with Maribel and invited her to come on as a guest. She accepted and invited me to the VaynerX headquarters in Manhattan. In addition to interviewing Maribel, she took me to Gary Vaynerchuk's office to meet him and get a selfie. I haven't interviewed Gary yet, but anything is possible!'

Andy's guests are a roll call of self-made entrepreneurs and champions, and have included Ryan Serhant who appears on Bravo's *Million Dollar Listing New York*, the creator of the exercise programme P90X, Tony Horton; Bill Courtney, whose football coaching story was told in the Oscar-winning documentary *Undefeated*; Nelson Dellis, the four-time USA Memory Champion, and four-time record-holding explorer Colin O'Brady. 'In looking back at my 150 episodes of *Inspired Money*, booking amazing guests requires the same consistent approach needed to create and produce a great show,' Andy wrote. 'This is not easy for independent, DIY podcasters like me who do not have a team. I tend to batch my outreach process by sending invitations out to people in the same week. While waiting for responses, I'll select appropriate guests who have reached out to me. It's definitely a balancing act, but you must keep asking.'

The promotional machine is an effective way for many subject-specific podcasters to schedule high-profile guests months ahead. The *My Dad Wrote a Porno* team and Jessie Ware on *Table Manners* deliberately avoid the promo tour and what can feel like a conveyor belt of celebrities peddling their goods across the mediascape at the same time. But for *Cooking the Books*, it's an efficient sell to the publicists organising a food writer's book tour. My listeners are niche; they're only interested in food and they only want to hear from the food writers at the top of their game. They want to know about their new books and to hear the authors talk about the thinking behind the food stories.

Emma Marjewicz is the head of publicity at a large publishing house in London. She told me that publicists looking to elevate their new book campaigns and reach their target audience are increasingly turning to podcasts as a way of doing this. 'Whilst broadcast is a great way to reach a wide demographic, we know audiences are shifting towards digital platforms. Podcasts are free, accessible and an easy way of honing in on specific areas of interest,' she emailed me. She told me that while TV and radio are the goal, it is also an extremely competitive area and the airtime given to an author is often very limited and usually dependent on topical features and news stories. 'Podcasts are a growing medium with more variety,' she said. 'Publicists like them because it allows for a more in-depth interview, the opportunity to explore the author's background, the context of the work and of course, actively plug the book. You can also better identify the podcasts ahead of time which will be relevant to the author, their field of work and also see the reviews from listeners. We want to hit the right audience and for there be an incentive for listeners to buy the book after the interview. Basically, we want book promotion to translate into book sales.'

Emma says that they look at a number of issues when deciding on which podcasts will be the most effective for their promotion:

- Will this podcast enhance an author's platform/increase their social media following at all?

- What is the podcast interviewer's background?
- How many interviews are on the podcast?
- Who has already been interviewed on the podcast?
- What are the podcast listening figures?
- Does the podcast have an audience that we want to tap into in order to further our outreach?
- How are people listening to the podcast? Can the podcast easily be streamed to an iPhone, iPad, tablet, etc.? Can it be found easily?
- Has the podcast received press coverage, reviews, recommendations?

Research your guests

Authors often prefer the more relaxed approach of a podcaster over being ferried into green rooms for a potentially stressful experience on camera. But Emma told me that it's important to make sure that the author is going to be comfortable with the format and interviewing style of the podcaster. She says that her team checks to see if the interview has an established format, how long it is – and whether the interviewer has a hidden agenda. They don't want the author to feel exposed if asked uncomfortable questions, and may ask for questions in advance. When I asked about this in the online communities, there was a mixed reaction. Some podcasters felt that they wanted to do everything they could to make their guest comfortable, while others reminded us that celebrities are human beings too and might prefer the fresher, looser feel. For *Cooking the Books,* I do it the other way around and ask my guests in advance for *their* four food moments from their latest book with a sentence on why. I then carve my skeleton script around their moments as *Desert Island Discs* would around the guest's choice of songs. It gives me a format that the publicists know well and which they can communicate to their author if they don't know the podcast, and it gives me a clear narrative arc to my show.

Research is everything and, in my experience, if you've done your homework, your guests will be humbled that you've taken the time to prepare properly. I find too that authors can enjoy being asked challenging questions if you know your subject; niche podcasters have a unique opportunity to share their passion with leaders in their field. Diana Henry wrote to my editor at *delicious.* after I interviewed her about her book *How to Eat a Peach* to say, 'I really do hope people listen to this, not for my sake but because it's so much better than the vast majority of podcast stuff out there. It's about food and IT'S PROPERLY SERIOUS.'

In the next chapter, we'll meet some of the podcasters whose mission is to meet their heroes and whose guests make their day – and who most of us will never have heard of. Welcome to the land of have-a-go-hobbyists, the bedrock of podcasting where it's not about the money.

POD POINTS

- Guests may need you as much as you need them
- Ask! You never know what might happen
- The publicity machine can work for you. Find out who the publicists are
- Play the long game: Doing your research on your guests will make for a better interview and a longer term relationship with the guest and the PR

6

The Niche Podcast: From Bedroom Hobby to Targeting Your Tribe

It's the star players and big hitters – the Joe Rogans and the Russell Brands – who may make the most noise about podcasting, but up and down the country lanes of Podcastland it's all about the niche, with clusters of communities doing their own thing, chatting about the ties that bind and adding a whole new dimension to what they love most. *Star Wars* enthusiasts enjoy a critique of their favourite films every single day with Alex Robinson and Pete the Retailer on *The Star Wars Minute* podcast, while *Game of Thrones* fans binge on *Pod of Thrones, Cast of Thrones, Game of Microphones* and any number of wittily named geek critiques of the HBO fantasy series. History nerds fill gaps in their education, music fans share vinyl finds and diversity podcasters create a world where their listeners no longer feel different. If you're a fan, podcasts are where you can find your tribe, where your hosts are your best friends and your fellow listeners are the only people who really understand you. You can hang out with them in the podcast's Facebook group, meet up at theme events and even appear on your favourite show. It's the fanzine of its day, the superfan's room of one's own, the sound of your daydreams. If you're the podcaster of a niche show and you've found your people, you're a superstar in your own world.

I posted a shout-out for favourite niche shows in Facebook Podcasters' Support Group, the 24,000-strong community of podcasters set up by podcasting champion Helen Zaltzman. It's a rich seam of niche hobbyists and big podcasters alike, and an excellent source of help. There was a deluge of responses. Peter Watson told me about his *Earth-2* podcast which explores the origins and development of the DC comics Multiverse and the legacy of Golden Age characters throughout the Silver and Bronze Ages of comics. 'We're working chronologically, covering stories that deal with parallel Earths and how DC editorial use that and their characters' rich history to tell new stories,' he wrote. Colin Jackson-Brown pointed me towards his podcast *Free With This Month's Issue* which he says himself is gloriously shambolic. But if you're one of the many blokes of a certain age obsessed with old free CDs from music magazines like *Kerrang!*, *NME* and *Melody Maker*, this is your place. Cynthia Bemis Abrams told me about *Advanced TV Herstory* which she says brings academic-level research and interviews about TV, women and culture; and Maggie Cubbler sent me to her *Unfiltered Journeys* podcast, which pairs her dual enthusiasms of self-improvement and beer. Steven Segaert embraces the small in his *De Vertaalpodcast* for Dutch-speaking freelance translators. 'To be fair, most of the content is interesting for freelancers in general also,' he wrote, 'but this is my crowd, so I'm having fun making it specific.'

The list was endless and took me on a psychedelic ride through Hibernian football (thanks to Euan McAleece for *Longbangers* and *Hibs Talk*), to early nineties Channel 4 game shows (*Under Consoletation*) and live-action Disney film (*Without A Mouse*). *Podcast 99* was a deep-dive, long-form investigation into what happened at Woodstock 99, while *Chart Music* had ex-*Melody Maker* journalists critiquing an episode of *Top Of The Pops* each week. But perhaps my favourite illustration of the niche podcast is Luke Miller's *Tile Money*, a show for tile installers about . . . tile installation. Sponsored by the National Tile Contractors Association in the US, it gets around 300 downloads per episode with over 100,000 plays over its first two years.

I had a brilliant response from Helen Ledwick who sent me a discreet email. 'I have a podcast about pelvic floor dysfunction – prolapse, incontinence, all the stuff that happens to your pelvic floor, especially after babies,' she wrote. 'It affects one in three women (including myself) but nobody ever talks about it. I get messages every day from women around the world thanking me for making them feel less alone and for giving them hope. It's an issue that most mothers can relate to to some extent. We are busting taboos for sure.' Its name? *Why Mums Don't Jump*.

Jon Wilks hosts the *Old Songs* podcast, a wonderfully niche show about British and principally English folk music from the archives at Cecil Sharp House, the headquarters of the English Folk Dance and Song Society (EFDSS) in London's Camden Town. A music journalist, storytelling is in Jon's DNA and the idea for the podcast, initially a blog, started with a romance. 'My uncle told me that my grandparents had met at this place called Cecil Sharp House,' he told me. 'This was in the late thirties and they'd "courted" there, going to cèilidhs. They loved dancing.' He discovered that his grandfather was a morris dancer and his grandmother a musician. 'I suppose as I was in my late thirties myself and getting towards that point where you start questioning where you come from a little bit more. It really fascinated me that there was this link to traditions and traditional music in my family that I had never known about before.'

Here's the moment where a podcast is conceived, even if Jon barely knew it himself at the time. An ocean of family stories was sitting in front of him, but the deep dive into the riches of folk and traditional English music could give him an audience with which to share the journey. This didn't have to be a solo passion project at all; on the contrary, he could become an expert in his field, leading his listeners by the hand into a whole new world of old songs.

He decided to teach himself about folk traditions and its music but with his journalist hat on, interviewing well-known folk musicians and writing a blog about what he found. 'A lot of people have written to me since and said that they got into traditional music because they read that blog,' Jon told me. But podcasting was becoming 'a bit of thing' in 2016 and he felt that it might be time to move on from the written word. 'These conversations are best heard rather than read,' he said.

And so, he did. In each episode of *Old Songs,* Jon explores one traditional song, looking at its origins and who would have sung it. He explained how it works: 'We've just done an episode on a song called Hal-an-Tow, which is traditionally sung in Cornwall on 8th May to welcome in the summer. And it's very, very heavily connected with May Day traditions. And so by talking about that song, naturally you start going off and thinking about what it means, what May means to this country: What people in the past would have done on a May morning, and that kind of thing.'

It's an archaeological dig into a community long gone, tracing its story about how the song itself has passed into folklore through various interpretations. For folk fans, it's a must-listen. 'I look at that song in the company of a well-known or prominent professional folk singer or traditional folk singer,' Jon explained. 'Nick Hart has been on it twice now. Jim Murray has been on it twice now. Through people like that then I've got bigger names like Billy Bragg who has been on it now.'

Other than Bragg, they're names that mean nothing to me, and that's the point. *Old Songs* podcast is not for me, and that's just fine by Jon. It's a perfect example of a passion podcast, a hobby that connects Jon to his community and provides a space for folk fans to feast on their favourite subject. He brings their heroes to them and they love him for it. Is it a huge audience? 'The podcast is still relatively young,' he told me, 'so it doesn't have vast figures. I think we get about 300 downloads per episode at the moment. But considering that the podcast is only, what, four months old, I think it's growing quite quickly. It's a good start.' Those 300 listeners are what the marketing people call hyper-engaged and valuable to the kind of sponsor who wants to talk directly to them. But Jon's day job is digital media and this, his passion project, is not for sale. 'I think if I was particularly bothered by engagement levels to the level that it was affecting what I was doing,' he said, 'then I feel like the podcast would lose something. I would start analysing it in far too much detail, and I'd start thinking, *Well, this has to go here, and this to fall here, and this has to fall here.* It's not a work project or anything like that, it's much more about getting the stories told, for me. I want those people to be able to come onto the podcast and not feel restricted by how things are supposed to be done. I want them just to be able to come on and really just enthuse about the music and the songs in the way that they want to do it.'

I asked him if there was a bite point where he has to have enough listeners to make it worth his while. If he wasn't getting any listeners, would there be any point in doing it? 'Ah, that's an interesting question,' he replied. 'I don't do this podcast to make money, but I do create content as a profession. So, I suppose if there was nobody listening then I would perhaps be a bit disheartened because I'm – this is going to sound terrible – but I'm slightly used to creating stuff that people listen to or look at. So, there would be an element of me that would think, *What's the point?* But fortunately, I'm not at that point.'

It may not be about the numbers for Jon, but for a hobby podcast like his there has to be a sense of expansion even if it is just in terms of knowledge. Hobbies are often about finding new facts, new things. They demand curation; for Jon, his podcast was about finding new old songs for his small but hungry audience. One of the challenges Jon encountered trying to build an audience for *Old Songs* is the use of music. The complicated British music licensing laws are stripped back to the only things you need to know as a podcaster in Chapter 8 (p.89), but the bottom line is: keep away from other people's music if you don't want to pay the price. If you want the might of iTunes nd Spotify to distribute your podcast and find your tribe, use copyright-free music from an agency like freemusicarchive.org or epidemicsound.com. For non-profit podcasters, mobygratis.com is a wonderful library of Moby tunes donated by the musician for free.

Jon publishes on Mixcloud which is not linked to Apple or Spotify or indeed any of the directories you need to build a large audience. But as Mixcloud partners with many of the largest rights holders, record labels and publishers around the world, its comprehensive licensing framework will cover your back and all rights holders, including the artists, will receive their royalties. Jon says it is 'massively frustrating. I didn't do my homework when I started doing this.' Before he realised the issue, he put a trailer out on Spotify for the show. 'And it got a lot of listeners, a lot of people who've since found me and said, why can't we find the rest of it? So, yes, hugely frustrating.'

He decided to get around the issue by asking his first guests to sing an unaccompanied version of the song, as traditionally it would have been sung. 'Traditional music would have been almost entirely unaccompanied,' he explained. 'Possibly a fiddle or a melodeon or something, but certainly not the sort of guitar thing that everybody thinks of now.' It's become part of the format: 'It's something that we end every podcast on now.'

But before music podcasters think they can negotiate the licensing laws by using their own version of any old music, Jon makes clear that it is just traditional music that is not copyrighted. 'This is probably the definition between what folk music is and what traditional music is,' Jon explained. Traditional music is anonymous. 'The song has developed of its own accord, almost like a sort of survival of the fittest. People have sung it in fields, in pubs, for years and years and it's been chipped away and it's been perfected by time, not by a specific person. And so, therefore there is nothing to copyright. Nobody can hold that copyright.' He gave me a famous example: 'Scarborough Fair', a traditional song that Paul Simon and Art Garfunkel made enormously popular in the sixties. 'Paul Simon took that arrangement and that song from Martin Carthy who is one of the most important traditional singers in this country, or any country really who sings in English – and Martin Carthy had taken that song from the archives, he'd made his own arrangement of it, ' Jon told me. 'And he'd arranged it in a way that people could potentially sing it again. But as far as Martin Carthy was concerned, he was just furthering the life of a song, supporting the tradition. It wasn't his song; this was just his version of it. Paul Simon took Martin Carthy's version and copyrighted it as his own and made millions off 'Scarborough Fair'. Martin Carthy's biggest gripe I think is not necessarily that he didn't have any money out of that. It's more that Paul Simon had the audacity to pretend that that song was something he'd written, which he clearly hadn't: it was a traditional song.'

It's a salutary tale of the complexities of music rights. Jon told me that all he wanted to do with this passion project was to 'further the life of those songs', and the way to do that is to get more people to hear them and to enjoy them. But it's not going to happen on Mixcloud on its own. He's made his peace: 'In the end I had to juggle that. I wanted the people whose arrangements I was using to get their royalties paid. Traditional musicians are not wealthy people by any means, so any little dribble that they can get is welcome. And I just weigh it up and think, well, if people are interested in it, then it's a click away. It just means they have to leave their desired app and go and listen to it somewhere else.'

TECH talk
Jon Wilks records *Old Songs* using Logic Pro X. His headphones are ATH-M20X by Audio Technica and he uses a Rode NT1 microphone.

New and Noteworthy and the niche
If the point of podcasting is about being part of the conversation, Jon

has become one of the leaders in his community of folk and traditional music. He has met his heroes and learned more about his passion. It's what niche podcasters do. But niche doesn't have to be small. Nicki Bannerman wanted to talk to the most inspiring women in the world, and so she did. She presents and produces *The Influential Women Podcast* with award-winning producer Juliette Nicholls and breakfast show producer Saffron Mirza. She explained why: 'We talk to inspiring women who have overcome their own challenges, from broadcasters and celebs to authors and campaigners who have thrived and survived setbacks, health and life challenges. We hear how they bounced back with resilience and wisdom to help others heal, thrive and move forward.' Guests have included Kirsty Young, the former presenter of BBC Radio 4's *Desert Island Discs*, Jane Garvey of BBC Radio 4's *Woman's Hour* and Judy Murray talking about her sons' Wimbledon Championships wins. Bannerman has chatted with Deborah Moggach, novelist and screenwriter of the *Exotic Marigold Hotel*, crime writer Clare Mackintosh and psychological thriller author Nicci Gerrard. As a freelance PR, marketeer, radio presenter and events producer, Nicki can indulge her fascination for uplifting life stories while making excellent contacts. 'We help change women's (and men's) mindsets, lives, hope and motivation and inspiration,' she told me. 'We have been described as "achingly human".'

Nicki wanted to get noticed and approached her podcast host Audioboom to see if they could help to get her show on iTunes' New and Noteworthy. It worked. I asked Amy Townley, global PR director at my own host, Acast, how to do it. She sent me the internal link used by her content team for submitting podcasts to Apple for consideration for New and Noteworthy. As I waded through the smoke and mirrors, I found the external link deep in Resources and Help on itunespartner.apple.com. I'm not sure it reflects the democratic spirit of podcasting, but fortune favours the brave in the world of podcasting, and sometimes if you ask, you get.

Value

Chris Hogg asked. The brain behind *Cassie and Corey* podcast takes us on an adventure into crowdfunding in Chapter 18 (p.167) and on the podcast *How to Grow a Pod*. He talked me through how he made sure that his wild musical comedy caper about eating disorders managed to get to New and Noteworthy within the vital first eight weeks, a time limit imposed by Apple to limit the selection to the newest of podcasts, and, presumably to encourage podcasters to put as much muscle into the launch as they can. He used LinkedIn to find the right person at iTunes, a mix of dogged determination, chutzpah and the penmanship of a professional playwright to win their hearts and minds. But it's the artwork that Apple demands that sorts the bedroom hobbyists from the professionals and the well connected. It's not the 4320 x 1080 pixels, 72 dpi and colour space of RGB that's the tricky bit but the delivery in an Adobe Photoshop PSD file. If you can make one yourself, you're halfway there. If you can't, you'll need to ask a very big favour of a graphic designer or splash some cash. This is time-consuming stuff. 'Ensure that talent, faces, and characters are layered to provide flexibility if edits need to be made by the Apple Design team,' writes Apple. 'Title treatments within the file must be on a separate layer, and scalable both up and down as a Photoshop "Smart Object" layer. Convert text to smart objects before transmitting them, not as text layers with editable fonts. Similarly, convert logos and title graphics to smart objects instead of providing simplified, or rasterized versions.' Entry to the world of podcasting is the easy part; entering the hallowed halls of New and Noteworthy, not so.

Cracking the charts

Lance Dann, co-author with Martin Spinelli of *Podcasting: the audio media revolution,* describes how he 'gamed the podcast system' with his ten-part drama series, *Blood Culture*, a 'hyperkinetic techno thriller' delivered across podcast, radio, film, blog and social media.

Lance is a former colleague at the University of Brighton whose interest in how it worked was academic but playful as he tested how to crack the algorithms and get the podcast to number 1 in the Apple Podcast charts.

His findings provide a blueprint for podcasters. While Apple deliberately obfuscate their methods of calculating their charts, Rob Walch of Libsyn told Lance some of its secrets for his 2017 book. 'The New and Noteworthy category is constructed from shows released in the past eight weeks and is based on a mixture of user reviews, ratings and subscriber numbers combined with some editorial oversight,' he writes. 'The chart itself is not based on the number of downloads a show receives in each period, but on the number of new subscribers it has.' Dann says that according to Walch, Apple has a formula based on the number of new subscribers on the day of the chart multiplied by four, plus the number of new subscribers on the previous day multiplied by three, plus the number of new subscribers two days ago multiplied by two, plus the number of new subscribers three days ago, plus four days ago, plus five days ago and then six days ago. Divide the total by thirteen, and you've got your Apple charts.

A wave of ennui passes over me, but Lance was on a mission for the sake of our students, or so I like to think. He worked it. He posted on Facebook a message to 'anyone who has ever known me or been taught by me, or has been married to me or been drunk with me or has fallen out with or been related to me, click this link and subscribe to my show.' He got five hundred subscribers on the first day of release which, he says, placed it next to Adam Buxton's podcast in the UK iTunes chart. Three days after launch, *Blood Culture* was number one in the Apple Podcast charts and had reached 150,000 listeners in just six months. Winning several industry awards was the icing on the cake.

Voices of the unheard

When *The Log Books* won Best New Podcast award at the British Podcast Awards in 2020, it was immediately catapulted onto New and Noteworthy as listeners piled in to hear why and created the all-important spike. 'In the three weeks since winning the award,' Adam Smith, one of its producers, emailed me after their win, 'we've seen a 180 per cent increase in downloads compared to the average number of downloads across three three-week periods prior to the award. We also received a fair amount of press coverage from the award including *Esquire, Metro, BBC Podcast Radio Hour, Evening Standard.*'

They too provided their logo as a PSD file to Apple, made by their graphic designer. They are thrilled with the success of the podcast but it wasn't the download figures that excited them. This is a passion project which created its own momentum. Radio producer Natasha (Tash) Walker is a volunteer for Switchboard, the second-oldest LGBT+ telephone helpline in the UK which first opened in 1974, and she chanced upon a rich seam of storytelling for what would become *The Log Books* podcast. I spoke to her and her colleagues Adam Smith and Shivani Dave a few weeks before they received the award about the extraordinary treasure trove which they have unearthed. 'We were moving the Switchboard archive to the Bishopsgate Institute,' Tash told me, 'and you just open it up and see all these hand-written notes, these memories, these stories. It's just jam-packed full of queer history, and you immediately fall right into it. You're laughing one minute and you're crying the next. And you can hear the voices. You can hear the emotions just falling off the pages. It just made sense to read them to catalogue them.' Tash, the radio producer, could already hear them. 'As I was doing it, I was thinking *This is audio*. Switchboard is a telephone helpline and information service, but it's also that connection. It's a spoken communication.' It felt like a no-brainer to make it a podcast. 'I love the intimacy of voice. There's something about listening, to music and radio and audio. It goes directly into your ears. It feels so connected to someone speaking directly into your ears. They're right there with you.'

But it was only when she was approached by podcaster Adam Smith while she was giving a presentation on her find for LGBT History Month, that the idea for *The Log Books* podcast was born. Adam had made his own podcasts about the history of desire among gay men in his spare time and had worked with the podcast team at his day job at *The Economist*. He approached Tash with the idea of doing a podcast together.

The podcast often features voices that you don't normally hear in podcasting, including older men and women who talk about being queer in the seventies and early eighties, and Shivani said that their Twitter page showed that younger people are coming to the podcast to learn about queer history. 'There's an inter-generational conversation between younger and older people who are talking to each other through the podcast. One of the moments that stands out was a heterosexual teacher said that *The Log Books* had educated her in ways that she had never understood before and that allowed her to better understand her LGBTQ students. We all felt very touched by that.'

It's been an organic growth, with Switchboard's own community sharing the podcast and word of mouth a key player. The team doesn't run a Facebook group or spend much time promoting it as they all have full-time jobs. Yet Adam said that since October 2019 when they launched, they're getting a very respectable 1000 downloads per episode with an all-time figure in July 2020 of 25,000. For a season of ten shows rather than a weekly, that's pretty good going, but with a BPA gold award under their belts, it is set to grow exponentially. As I chatted to them a month before their surprise win, Shivani said, 'It's not about getting to number one. It's a passion for all of us. It's not about the size of the audience; it's about getting the stories out there.'

<u>**TECH** talk</u>
Adam records on H4N, using Sound link 3 headphones, an Mpm1000 Marantz mic and a mic stand borrowed from a neighbour. He edits on Adobe Premiere and uses the video too for social media. Acast is the podcast's host.

The niche community

Suzy Buttress had been an avid podcast listener for thirteen years by the time she first started *The Casual Birder* podcast in November 2017. 'I've been a birdwatcher since I was a kid,' she told me. 'I just really enjoyed being around birds. I'm not one of those birders that go out on expeditions to find a particular rare bird. I take my birding where I find it.'

Her passion for her subject is contagious and in the niche world of birding, Suzy is a humble leader – thanks to her podcast. I asked her if, like most podcasters, she suffered from imposter syndrome when she launched her first episode into her community of equals. 'I was thinking, *Why would anyone listen to me?* But she was bursting to talk about birding to people who shared her passion. 'I had already been thinking about doing a series of talks at local clubs and groups,' she told me.

She knew that she couldn't rely on friends and family to listen – nor did she want to. In fact, her ambition was tiny: 'I didn't really expect anyone to listen week by week. I thought at the beginning it would be nice if it found someone.' With no intention to earn any money from the podcast, she admits to not having any plan at all. 'I had so much material that I had been recording anyway that I thought, *Well why not put it out there and it might become a little legacy for me so if I'm not around, my friends and family could then listen if they wanted to.*'

Ah, the funeral theory of podcasting. Well, why not? Who

doesn't secretly write their funeral speech? But Suzy's mourners may well turn out to be a much wider and more fascinating community than she might have imagined in those early days. In the cosy world of niche podcasting, friends are easily made, even if you're not in the same niche. It seems that it was a community of practice that Suzy was looking to connect with rather than simply finding fellow birders, and they came through the love of podcasting itself.

Networks were the key to Suzy's success, both on and offline. She set about meeting up in London with podcast listeners whose tastes were similar to her own. 'I got a lot of support from friends in the wider podcasting community,' she told me, 'so I thought there might be a couple of friends there who might listen and they might have relatives who are interested in birds so they could suggest having a listen.' But by joining the listener community of Maximum Fun, a network of comedy and culture podcasts, she became an active member of relatively early adopter listeners who would pay anything between £5 and £100 per month to wear the T-shirt. Literally. As Olly Mann says in Chapter 16 (p.158), fans want to support their heroes, and Maximum Fun gives them a way to 'empower and enable the creators who enrich their lives'. Like fans of Olly's podcast *The Modern Mann*, MaxFun's community is described (by MaxFun) as 'incredibly intelligent, passionate, and compassionate', with 'a desire to make the world a better place', and fans, through their regular donations, support Los Angeles Regional Food Bank, the National Immigration Law Center, the National Court Appointed Special Advocate (CASA) Association, Southern Poverty Law Center, the American Foundation for Suicide Prevention. Membership of MaxFun gave Suzy and thousands of other podcasting fans a niche community which had a sound and a purpose. It felt good to belong.

Its podcasts include MaxFun's founder's *Bullseye with Jesse Thorn* which was originally conceived as *Sound of Young America* in 1999 when Thorn was a sophomore at UC Santa Cruz. It became the network's original podcast way back in 2004. With more than half a million listeners currently tuning in to MaxFun's forty podcasts including the cult classic, *Beef And Dairy Network Podcast* and *Star Trek* favourite *The Greatest Generation,* it distributes its shows via National Public Radio (NPR). As podcasting's popularity has taken off, they have grown their team substantially, while still managing to retain their niche network flavour. 'Making something that has a powerful appeal to a small group of people is almost always better than a good appeal to a large group of people,' Jesse Thorn told the *LA Times* in 2018. 'Never in a million years could there be a radio station or even radio show based solely on *Star Trek,*' Thorn told reporter Hayley Fox. 'If you make something that really is important to people, even if it's important in an unusual or specific or niche way, then you are touching their lives much more powerfully than just creating a perfectly okay sitcom, for example. That is what we're always trying to do.'

Suzy's membership of MaxFun's listener community opened the door to a world of podcasting, inviting her into the unofficial Slack group for MaxFun fans in which she could make new friends, many of whom were podcasters too. She even flew to a MaxFunCon event in California, an annual three-day gathering of creatives led by the network where, like something out of a Hollywood movie, the British birder from Basingstoke was sprinkled with podcasting fairy dust by her heroes, podcasting pioneers who would change her destiny by inviting her in to their gang. 'I met Lance Anderson from *Verge of the Fringe,* and Harry Durran from *Podcast Junkies,*' she told me, blushing slightly. 'Harry's a fantastic guy.' He had already invited her on to his show as a guest by the time they met in LA. 'Every now and then, something will pique his interest,' she laughed. She had told him on Twitter that she hosted a birding podcast and 'as there weren't many around, he interviewed me and put it out! That was so amazing because he has had a lot of well-respected people on his show. It immediately made me feel that my show was worth listening to, that there's someone out there who doesn't know me and has no invested interest in me as a person but who thinks my show sounds interesting and wants to interview me.'

In Los Angeles she was hanging out with Harry, Lance Anderson and Eric Trules from *e-travels with e. trules* podcast, 'famous' names in the small pond of podcasting, and Suzy was enchanted. 'He's travelled the world,' she flushed. 'I met them in the afternoon at the reception party and then in the evening, Lance put together this meet-up of all these original podcasters. I felt as a new podcaster quite overawed, but it was a really wonderful experience because it made me feel like I could be a part of this community. It gave me such confidence.'

Unlike the more transient celebrity of Instagram, podcasting is an enabling medium which lets its newcomer share the stage. This brush with the big guys that Suzy describes so well can open doors if you've got something to say and the drive to do it well. It's a *quid pro quo*; taking your hobby seriously and doing well drives up the quality of podcasting per se. It adds status to other podcasters who will often generously pass around the opportunity to help each other to raise their game.

Suzy was hobby-fishing in a small but fertile pond where the etiquette was to listen and support each other, and, where appropriate, to appear on each other's show, sharing communities and growing each other's audiences. 'I had a few people early on who enjoyed the show and were happy to support it by tweeting about it and telling their networks and then it grew from there.' And not a birder among them. 'That was all from the podcast side not the bird side,' she said. 'That's only come much later.'

She did the same, mentioning her favourite shows on podcaster support groups, on her show and to her podcast listening community, never asking for anything and quietly getting it. It's the giver's gain protocol, the generosity of giving without expecting a return. The universal law of attraction. Suzy says that she's simply interested in other people. 'I have no expectation that people will say, "I'll definitely talk about your show".' The Facebook podcast groups work on the same principle with pioneers like Helen Zaltzman and the *Answer Me This!!* team giving back to the endless stream of new podcasters lining up to ask the same questions. Admins redirect them to the search bar while podcasters old and new bolster the occasionally disheartened and share their failures in a show of solidarity. It's social networking at its most human.

And it works: Suzy's *Casual Birder* is now in the top 20 per cent of British podcasts in terms of downloads. She won't reveal how many that is but says that according to Libsyn, her hosting company, 'If you're getting more than 147 listeners per episode, you're doing as well as half the other podcasts out there. But then it jumps very quickly. If you get around 1400 listeners in the last thirty days, you're in the top 10 per cent of podcasts. But then it jumps massively so if you're getting 3500 or more, it jumps very high.'

It's taken her three years to get there, and she's happy with the result. As Jason Allan Scott says in Chapter 15 (p.149), you only need one thousand fans who will follow you anywhere. Suzy enjoys the leverage it gives her to become a birding expert, to appear occasionally on her local BBC station and to justify the enormous amount of time she invests in making the podcast while holding down a day job. 'I was fortunate enough to be asked in to do several sessions of hour-long interviews on a Sunday afternoon show that deals with cooking, gardening, nature, so I thought I'm absolutely here speaking to the audience that I need to speak to.' With an average age of 60 plus, BBC local radio is not (yet) the home of podcast listeners, and her appearances have not created a spike in her download figures. But Suzy could use this to further leverage her expert status on other platforms and drive new fans back to her podcast.

Podcasters are rarely born; they are made, and examples like Suzy's are evidence that the most humble of show hosts can take what they want from the experience. Suzy says that she is not in it for the money but the sheer joy she receives from podcasting is palpable and inspiring. By day, she is a project manager and says that she has none of the 'entertainment' genes that underscore the success of many of the podcasting pioneers who tell their stories in this book and on its podcast. She puts her success down to being an early adopter: 'I had business cards made up to hand out to people if I was in conversation with them, so they could go and look it up if they wanted to. But only two years ago, a lot of people still didn't really know what a podcast was. The explosion has really happened in the UK in the last couple of years.'

She doesn't have a big following on Twitter, but she does put time into the Facebook group. Again, because she's the genuine enthusiast, it works. 'I have my Facebook group but I also do an engagement thing every week on Twitter and Instagram called "What Bird Wednesday?",' she told me. 'I use photographs which either I've taken or listeners have sent to me for the purpose. Earlier on in the day I will show a portion of the photograph that had clues in it in terms of plumage details, or I'll tell you where it might be found. Or it might have a similar size to something else you might know but it's like an investigation thing. If you know the bird, tell me and if you don't know it, have a go or look it up in a guide and see if you can work it out.' Later in the day, she returns to post the full photograph 'so people can see whether they were right or not'. It's competitions like this which engage the audience, whether they listen to the podcast or not. 'We've got people who take part, but those people communicate with me as a result of the photo and don't necessarily listen to the show. So, you start to build different types of communities with people who are interested in what you're doing but not necessarily in your show. Which is a bit strange but it's all interest.' And interest means engagement. Engagement means followers and followers means influence. From there, it's up to you to leverage whatever you like. Or not.

Facebook works best for Suzy, but it does take time, something that she is happy to give. After speaking to her, I tried it out. My aim: to create more of a community for *Cooking the Books* with plenty of chat between listeners via a Facebook group. Each week, I write a post with a link to the latest episode of the podcast, but I quickly noticed that it was my usual Facebook crowd who liked or posted something supportive. It's my Instagram followers who are less likely to be people I know and whose comments feel like they're genuinely interested in the content. I could – and should – build on my existing Facebook friends to grow a stronger community in the group, posting different content to my Instagram feed. I could post the recipes that I try out as part of my interview prep, showing the group inside the books I podcast about in a way that I don't on Instagram. But for me, it just feels like a moment too long on social media. I'd rather go for a walk in the woods. The joy of running my own show is that I can change gear as and when I want to. According to Buzzsprout's 2020 stats, *Cooking the Books* is heading towards the top 5 per cent of podcasts after just six months and I can take my foot off the accelerator a little now. Perhaps the satisfying interactions of a genuine community group are among the rewards on the long cruise ahead.

TECH talk

Suzy uses a Zoom H6 for general recording with an AKG D5 mic and has an H1 with a setting for cutting wind noise for outdoor use, sometimes attaching a Rode SmartLav lapel mic. On a really windy day, Suzy uses a Movo WS-G9 furry outdoor windscreen muff for her lapel mic which she plugs into her Zoom H1. She edits on Hindenburg.

<<<Listen to the whole interviews with Jon Wilks, the team behind The Log Book *and Suzy Buttress on* How to Grow a Pod. *>>>*

POD POINTS

- Niche is the heartland of podcasting. The global average is 147 downloads per episode
- Put your passion in your podcast and the rest will follow
- Be the leader of your tribe
- Build a community on social media but check your motivation
- Join support networks where you can meet other podcasters

7

The Network

Podcasting can be a solitary activity. It is ideally suited to freelancers who have the drive, ideas and resilience to make their own work and to keep it going when the chips are down, but it can be lonely. We may long for the camaraderie of the team but we get more done by ourselves and steer clear of the office politics. So, when there's a drink with other podcasters down the road on offer, it's hard to refuse.

But walking into a party of strangers is hard, however much of an interest you share, and I took a couple of girlfriend podcasters with me for company when I ventured into my first podcasters' meet-up at Kings Place at the back of London's Kings Cross. 'Look for the headphone hair,' wrote Helen Zaltzman, one of the first podcasters in the UK and the organiser of the meet-up. We spotted a lone woman wandering a little aimlessly with suspiciously frizzy locks, and asked her if she was looking for the podcasters' meet-up. She was. We bought some drinks and chatted, trying to make ourselves heard in the busy post-work bar until someone spotted Helen. Again we chatted amiably, and asked how many people she was expecting. 'They're already here,' she told us and pointed to the tables, the bar stools, the people gathered outside. 'They're all podcasters.'

Helen has become known as the matriarch of British podcasting, largely because she was among the very first in the country, but also because of her role in supporting and teaching others about the industry. Her TED Talks, Radio Academy panel discussions and frequent appearances in the media have made her the go-to person on podcasting, but it's her meet-ups and Facebook supporters' group which have won her the most affection among the community itself. Her regular calls for members to sign up to for cross-promos with other podcasters in the group is a useful resource, and a reminder of how a community of like-minds can and should help itself.

You can listen to the full interview with Helen on *How to Grow a Pod*, in which she told me why she put so much energy into spreading the word back in 2014 when podcasting had yet to boom in the UK. 'People wanted to learn how to do it,' she told me. 'There still weren't masses of resources out there.' She was outraged when she heard about an organisation that was charging for meet-ups: 'I felt that it was really against the spirit of what I think it should be, particularly when you're a beginner. Most people are not making money at the start of the podcast and may never do so. There are so many barriers to entry to doing a creative thing and I wanted to remove as many of those as possible. And one of those is financial or the feeling that there's a lot of information you don't have access to. There's actually not that much that you need to know. I didn't know much when I started, and there wasn't much guidance around. We had to figure it out ourselves.'

People were already asking her for podcasting advice for free in regular café surgeries. When Roman Mars, podcast pioneer, host and producer of *99% Invisible*, and a founder of the podcast collective Radiotopia, of which Helen is a member, was in London, she organised an event. 'That was quite a busy meet-up and the best thing about it ... was just seeing people meet each other and spark off each other. And some of them started working together. That was really wholesome.'

The Facebook group has grown exponentially, with 24,000 members all over the world as I write. Helen and her husband Martin Zaltz Austwick are among seven moderators who keep the peace. But they also stimulate discussions; after Gimlet Media was sued for not making their podcasts accessible to the deaf and hard of hearing,

Helen posted: 'What kinds of things do you do to make your show more accessible? Transcripts for deaf and hard of hearing people? Making sure your website works for blind people using screen readers? Ensuring no flashing images? What else? Any useful advice, resources and techniques you can share?' Drama podcaster Fiona Thraille was among the ninety to comment: 'We put up transcripts, and for audio drama, it's very usual to pan voices to the left and right, especially when someone is entering or leaving a scene. After reading comments on a group by someone with hearing loss in one ear, I now make sure not to pan anything too far because otherwise for anyone with hearing loss on one side, the dialogue can completely disappear.'

The group is an essential resource. 'You can ask about any little tips for anything,' said Helen. 'I'm constantly popping in there and finding answers to stuff. It can be very tacky and very nerdy and very broad ranging and very existential. A lot of it is boring but sometimes you think, *Wow, I'm really glad someone voiced that thought and that I got to see it.*'

The group feels like a celebration of podcasting (although Helen told me that I should see the back end to get a feel of what it's really like) and gives us an idea of where it's heading. 'I feel like British podcasting is a few years behind the US,' Helen told me. She thinks this is due to the strength of our radio output which offers good audio storytellers and journalists a sustainable career, something which separates us from the more entrepreneurial spirit of America. 'They're like, "I'm going to do a thing",' she said. 'Whereas in Britain, we're like, "I'm not going to work unless you make me." There's a lot of things at play that are cultural, but also structural.'

Since 2007, when Helen first launched *Answer Me This!!* with Olly Mann, there has been an enormous growth in podcasting and more competition for people's 'ear time'. She believes that a significant shift occurred with the introduction of the news podcast, and in particular with *The Daily* in 2017, a news podcast from the *New York*

Times hosted by political journalist Michael Barbaro which features interviews with its cast of reporters. 'When *The Daily* started in the wake of the Trump election,' she said, 'it suddenly meant that people's ears were committed to just one show for that commute every day rather than five different shows a week.' Time became an issue suddenly; while podcasts had predominantly covered anything other than current affairs, with *The Daily* it evolved into an opportunity to go deeper into the news of the day. We saw the same with *Brexitcast*, *Newscast* and other podcasts from BBC Sounds in particular, which became essential and daily listening for those obsessed with the news of the day. 'It was a shift artistically,' said Helen, 'but I think in listener behaviour too.'

The hub

Networking in real life, sharing stories and supporting each other as you develop your podcast, is the unusually sociable part of podcasting life, but teaming up with a podcasting hub, an online community of practice, can feel like being part of a working team. Cressida Ward and Daniel Levine have created a community of content creators on FoodTryb.com, a micro-influencer community and content creation site which may one day rival Instagram, where creators in the food and drink space can be found under one roof. As we post our podcasts, publish recipes and post the pictures behind our stories, the idea is to share an income from brand partnerships while making new friends with influence. I've joined up and you can hear more from Cressida and Daniel on *How to Grow a Pod* in a 'before and after' analysis of my own participation. 'We're all about empowering the smaller creators,' Daniel told me. 'There's tons of people – celebrity chefs, big YouTubers with millions of followers, but there's also everyday people who do it full time or part time who want to create frequently and participate in the conversation.' 'It could be a mum,' said Cressida, 'it could be a working cook. They might have a few thousand followers, a few hundred. It doesn't matter. We want a place for them, to have a community. We're essentially putting our arm around smaller creators and giving them more strength in numbers really.'

Cressida and Daniel, who co-present the *Food Tryb* podcast, both come from advertising backgrounds and work with brands at the company. The community is a clever opportunity to get to know their creators better through workshops events and support, engaging with them and understanding how best to work with suitable brands if appropriate. 'We want people who are in the food space who can bring interesting stories to the table, literally,' said Daniel.

It's a tempting idea, and one that I see evolving into an online/offline world of content creators mentoring and supporting each other to get the most out of the world of social media. The age of the bedroom hobbyist may be on the wane as lone podcats gather to prowl together and pick up the titbits of a podcasting culture increasingly dominated by celebrities and sponsorship deals. As audiences grow and content creators as well as more traditional presenters come into the podcasting space, so the brands take their place at the feast. Food Tryb is already unfolding its napkin. 'I think that traditional media such as TV and radio will start having their own shows,' Cressida told me. 'Look at how everyone has a YouTube channel. If you're a presenter on a TV show, you should have your own podcast. You own the content. You own the direction of the channel.' Celebrities like Fearne Cotton and Russell Brand are already there. 'I think that's what podcasting will become,' Cressida said, 'because if you're a radio host and you worked for one of the big networks, why shouldn't you? Why doesn't their agent get a brand, put them on their own podcast, upload it themselves in their own time? They'd be investing in the talent. I think talent will have more power.'

We'll read a discussion with Josh Adley about the growth in brand sponsorship in the next section, and it follows that this has brought an influx of celebrities into the entertainment space as well as drama. 'I think a lot of celebrity-fronted podcasts have been dominating the market,' said Helen Zaltzman, 'and maybe it's good in that it will get people in who weren't listening to podcasts before, or they were like, "I've never heard of it, but then this major TV channel is doing them so maybe that's something I can comprehend". But again, it makes it harder for people like me who were nobodies in the living room to reach people's ears.'

A celebrity presenter does not always make a winning podcast either; Helen reminded me that Spotify paid Amy Schumer a million dollars to present a podcast which failed to attract many listeners. But it does change the shape of the space when celebrities begin to dominate. I gave Helen the example of the *delicious.* podcast sharing the top spot in the food podcast charts with *The Food Programme* most weeks in 2016, even knocking Radio 4's long running serial *The Archers* off the top spot on one occasion in the Arts charts until the appearance of *Table Manners with Jessie Ware* in 2017. It was largely Jessie Ware's own media sensibility and pop star content that made it an instant hit, but it certainly relegated *the delicious.* podcast (and all the other food podcasts apart from the mighty *Food Programme*, with its forty-year legacy) to the subs bench in the food charts. Helen told me that it's still down to the listener. 'You need to pitch it to the listener every single time, why it will be a good use of their time because they have so much other internet to be entertained by. So why would they stay?' She says that good old-fashioned press coverage will make all the difference, and *Table Manners* is still counting its column inches. 'In the case of Jessie Ware, it's a different kind of leverage to get coverage in old media. Old media does still make a difference in getting podcasts listeners.'

Now you've got the basics. You've decided what you've got to say and how to say it. You know how to book your guests, speak to your tribe and find your network. In the next chapter we'll get technical with the knobs and buttons behind podcasting. Ready? Press Play.

TECH talk

Helen records on a Zoom H6. The mic she was using for our interview was a Shure SM7B but her current regular mic is a Rode NTG4 shotgun. She edits on Logic.

POD POINTS

- Join an online podcast support group
- Consider joining a hub
- It's always down to the listener

8

The Kit List

What kit do I need? It's among the first questions anyone who wants to get into podcasting will ask, but very possibly the least interesting subject, for me at least in this colourful, DIY world of the pod. There are more books on this than you need in your life, and this isn't one of them. Like many of my podcasting colleagues, I use a Zoom H4N microphone, which captures sound excellently, and I use just the one editing software, Pro Tools. I have one pair of headphones, Beyerdynamic DT 990 Pro, and the rest is inside my head.

Sound

In terms of a studio, I use a duvet over my head to record my links. I've got a pile of soundproofing curtains in my barn which maybe, by the time I finish this book, I will have hung up to create a sound booth. But then again, life may be too short to bend a curtain rail. Helen Zaltzman and Olly Mann both used padded backdrops when I interviewed them for this book and its accompanying podcast (Helen's was a quilt over a clothes rail), and most of my interviewees made do with a carpeted floor with plenty of soft furnishings to mop up the sound of space. You'll see what they use to record their podcasts at the end of their stories, and if you want to talk tech, there are a million geeks populating the podcasting support groups on Facebook desperate to feast on the subject, should you ask. Personally, I'm much more interested in what the tech can do with the talk.

Microphones

When I was first invited to produce the *delicious.* podcast in 2016, I was interviewing my soon-to-be boss, Seamus Geoghegan of Eye to Eye Media, on an iPhone with a plug-in Zoom microphone which quite literally plugs into the bottom of your phone. It did the trick, both in terms of capturing Seamus for another project on a gorgeous summer day among the hustle and bustle of Borough Market, and in getting me the job of my dreams. 'Do you know what to do with that?' he asked me. I checked the levels were between -6 and -12 decibels. 'Yup,' I said. And I did.

I even recorded my very first episode using that mic, each story captured while out and about, one even on a motorbike as I was sped around the island of Spetses by my local Airbnb host in search of horta, the spinach-like weeds that grow on the cliffs overlooking the Mediterranean, sprinkled with pine leaves from the trees above and washed with the salt spray of the ocean. With that tiny mic plugged into my iPhone, I not only captured the simple but utterly delicious pleasure of being adopted by a local food-lover but, quite by accident, the binaural Doppler effect of his motorbike shifting from right ear to left as he sped off after dropping me home. The podcast geeks loved that. I didn't even notice.

When I moved up from an iPhone Zoom mic to Zoom H4N, I joined the pros. Hana Walker-Brown, whose podcasts are works of art, has been recognised and awarded internationally for her work over the last decade. Her documentaries use technology to give her unprecedented access into the deepest, darkest depths of human beings and their lives. Her work is compelling, internal, using the medium to get inside our heads to tell stories of underdogs and amplify the voices of the misrepresented or silenced. If you think she needs more than a Zoom H4N to do that, think again. Hana, like me, has only ever used an H4N and has no intention of looking elsewhere. 'It's like my extra limb. It's almost like I'm doing this dance with it in my hand, which sounds really wonky and ridiculous, but that's just how I've learned to use it,' she told me. 'I think I have an attachment to it because I've made every single doc and podcast I've ever done on this.' I know how she feels; when *delicious.* asked for the Zoom I'd been using for four years at the end of our tenure, it was like asking me to rip my own arm off. Hana explained that for her, an interview was like putting an arm around her contributor. Unlike me, she prefers not to use the handle which she compared to holding a gun, using the machine as an extension of her arm. Georgia Catt, producer of *The Missing Cryptoqueen*, did the same, but while Hana's intention was to make the process of capturing the audio invisible and forgotten, enabling the experience for both interviewer and interviewee to be precious and intimate, Georgia's was about safety. At the bizarre Miss OneCoin beauty pageant in Romania, security staff and OneCoin's dodgy inner circle had been alerted to the BBC investigation team within their midst, so recording with a Zoom meant being able to keep it almost literally up her sleeve.

The mantra in any audio is 'record the best sound at source'. There's very little you can do once you've got the wav. file into your editing software, so it's vital to get it right in the moment. And it's easy enough; there's a very low entry level to podcasting. With a good microphone like a Zoom, you just need to check that your recording levels are between -6 and -12 decibels, that you're not 'popping' by talking too close to the mic (a good tip is to talk over the top of the mic to avoid the plosives, the S and P sounds that explode in the ear) and use a windsock, particularly if it's windy. The rest is about the story. But that's the DIY approach of the podcaster. I remember the quizzical expression on the face of a Radio 4 producer when I was introduced as one of the nominees up against her for an award. We chatted about the stride of the podcast into ground once only occupied by the BBC. 'But,' she stammered, 'what about the quality?' And it's true that with just a £200 recording device with built-in microphone, I couldn't begin to achieve what her team could. But that wasn't the point. The point of the *delicious.* podcast was to take the listener by the hand, and in the spirit of podcasting, to find the hole in the wall, and with a quick look over the shoulder, duck down and lead them to another land where their favourite food folk live. This is where the smell of freshly baked cake fills the air, where Raymond Blanc is building a bee village just down from where Nigella and Ottolenghi are chatting about how they became single-name food heroes. Where Gill Meller is baking a mackerel on firewood found on a Jurassic beach and Rick Stein is reaching down to help the lobster catch in from the boats. It's a land of pluck and chutzpah and it should sound that way. I am no Radio 4 producer but, like the *delicious.* listener, I am an interloper with an invitation to tea. Editing it all together on my laptop afterwards should be like opening my bag to chuckle at the cake I nicked when no one was looking.

And that's the fun of it. With the lowest of tech and often solitary location work, you have to be inventive. I've had Rick Stein inside my vast winter coat as a wind break against the breeze off Padstow quay, much to the lusty guffaws of passing fishermen. Angela Hartnett and I have stood bosom to (larger) bosom with my faux fur protecting us against the elements, and getting super-close to Jamie Oliver and Massimo Bottura to shield against the clatter of their busy work spaces around us added an intimacy that I hadn't planned. When the chips are down, there's always another way. Anything less is a failure of the imagination.

Podcasting kit checklist

At the end of each of the stories from the podcasting pioneers littered throughout this book, you can read their kit list, but here's a user-friendly, get-up-and-go rundown of the basics.

- Portable recording device with SD card

- Windsock: If you're recording outside, a windsock is essential. Placed over the mic, it can reduce much of the sound of wind and external noise. I use a foam windsock for everyday recording and the fabulously named Dead Kitten windsock for recording outside, which has transformed my sounds of the seaside, recordings on boats, etc.
- Good headphones. Over the ear noise-cancelling earphones are a must
- Laptop
- Mic with USB capability that can plug into your laptop for host reads (optional if you have a portable device and a soundproofed room or duvet)
- Mic stand (optional if you're using a portable device)
- The option of plugging one or two other mics into your laptop for guests in your 'studio'
- Software to record directly to your laptop and software to edit and mix (add music, etc.) with (optional)
- Soundproof studio or duvet. I've used a duvet over my head to record my links since I started podcasting. It's the easiest form of soundproofing and one that was adopted by Fearne Cotton among many other radio hosts and celebrity podcasters who couldn't get to their studios during lockdown. Add carpet and curtains and as many soft furnishings as you can to absorb sound. And if you're really serious, you can stick soundproofing panels to your wall. Cover them with soundproofing curtains for an inexpensive and efficient way of creating a home sound studio
- Laptop bag: When I'm recording on location, I take a backpack containing my laptop and USB to SD card lead in case my SD card needs offloading. If you can't take that much kit with you, at least take a memory stick and lead. To avoid a full SD card, adopt a good housekeeping habit of filing your audio on your laptop after each recording session

- Spare batteries
- Smartphone. Increasingly, smartphones are offering great quality, and, with a voice recording app, like Voice Memos or Handy Rec can be an excellent back-up or option to the more professional portable devices

Editing software

This is where the magic happens. Although what you capture at source is essential to the quality of your podcast, it's in the edit suite on your laptop where you can really craft your story, adding music and effects, layering it with links and playing with as much or as little as you want. A simple clip-and-link podcast, in which the audio illustrates the story while the narrator explains the context, echoes the format of most BBC storytelling and news reports since the broadcaster first set the gold standard, and this is one of the easiest ways of telling your story on a multi-layered editing system. It's also where you can break the rules. But first, you'll have to learn them.

Recording properly at source is essential to a good end product, and unless you're savvy with sound, it'll save you a headache if you follow the simple rules. Check your recording levels are between -6 and -12 decibels, talk over or under the mic to avoid popping and hissing sounds, use a windsock in the wind and move your mic to the mouth that's speaking – and nine times out of ten, you should be fine. As Helen Zaltzman says, it's a very low entry level into podcasting.

But if, as we enter a new era of social distancing, quarantines and nationwide lockdowns, you're relying on your guest to record their own audio while you chat over Zoom, you may find that your clear instructions to avoid talking directly into the mic may have been misunderstood. It happened to me as I directed the young food ambassadors for the *Right2Food* podcast via Zoom. I should have asked them to record a section of the script using Voice Memos on their phones and email it to me to check the levels, but I didn't. For the most part it was fine, but occasionally the sound was so muffled that it was unusable. With no time to organise another Zoom to redo it, I called in Small Paul, sound man to the stars. If he couldn't unmuffle my young presenter, no one could.

'I just gave it a bit more on the top end,' he said when I asked him how he had delivered such crystal-clear sound in a matter of minutes. In a world of sound frequencies, my young ambassador's voiceover had barely any as he tried so hard to avoid hissing into his mic that he virtually pushed it into his throat. Paul described the sound as muffled with a 'boxiness' that came from recording in a room that would have benefited from soft furnishings to absorb the sounds. But, with the magic of Pro Tools' audiosuite, which comes as standard, he selected EQ-7, which gave him seven 'bands', or points, along the frequency from low to high to drag and play with until he had found enough treble to open up the sound and have our young presenter enunciating like a pro.

Paul explained that while he was amplifying the treble on this occasion, EQ can also deal with boomy sounds by dragging the band down to remove the bass. A thin and weedy sound can be boosted by giving it more bass. Open up the audio suite on your editing software and play around to see what can be achieved.

I use Pro Tools because I've always done so. It's not the cheapest but it's easy, efficient and does everything I need it to do. But for those who come to my classes and retreats, I recommend the free audio software Audacity or GarageBand first.

Popping into the Podcasters' Support Group to find what the current suggestions are in the regular threads about favourite editing software, the most popular are:

- Hindenburg (£79)
- Pro Tools (£20 monthly subscription)
- Adobe Audition (£23 monthly subscription)

- Reaper (£48)
- Logic Pro (£79) or Logic Pro X (£299)

Ira Glass and Chris Hogg told me about an astonishingly effective addition to editing called Descript, which transcribes your audio and enables you to edit the words or the audio. It may well revolutionise the editing process. It's offered in tiers from free for up to three hours of transcription to $15/month for unlimited.

Podcast host Buzzsprout has a fully updated checklist on equipment, as do many of its competitors, and adds one more to the top five:

- Alitu: The Quick & Easy Way to Make your Podcast ($28/month)

LUFS

For a low-tech podcaster like me, the idea of mastering my shows to make them Spotify-ready is a no-no, and happily there's another website, Auphonic, that will do it for a small fee. All you need to know is that after you've finished your edit, converted it into an mp3 or wav. file, you'll need your show to have the right LUFS (Loudness Unit Full Scale). Spotify explains why you need to master your file on its website: 'Audio files are delivered to Spotify from distributors all over the world and are often mixed/mastered at different volume levels. We want to ensure the best listening experience for users, so we apply Loudness Normalization to create a balance.' Spotify has recently changed its LUFS to -14 decibels which Auphonic will automatically master for you. It's free for 2 hours of processed audio per month and around £10 per month if you need more. Soundcloud and Buzzsprout have just added an option to master your files, and by the time you read this, most hosts will probably do the same. Check with your host using their support email or chat bot to find out.

Podcasting hosts

Once you've made your show and put it through Auphonic, it's time to upload it to your podcast host. Distribution is the essential but super-techy end of podcasting where your audio files are stored, your RSS feed is created and how your show is distributed. It's the engine room of podcasting, and the bit I'm more than happy to pay for someone else to do.

But which hosting company to choose is one of the much-discussed subjects in any of the online podcast communities. PodBean, Spreaker, Anchor, Buzzsprout and Podomatic are all among the most popular hosts who have a free entry level, while Libsyn, Blubrry and Acast Open offer good deals for a small monthly payment of around £10.

If you're a celebrity or brand and are likely to bring in a huge audience which will attract sponsorship, you may even get your hosting for free. The *delicious.* podcast and Leon's *How to Eat to Save the Planet* are hosted by Acast, the Swedish company which launched in 2014 with, in the words of co-founder Johan Billgren, a mission to 'take creators from bedroom heroes to worldwide success stories'. With its marketing and sales support 'across an open podcasting ecosystem', Acast quickly became one of the biggest names in podcast hosting with huge shows like *My Dad Wrote a Porno* and *Table Manners with Jessie Ware* getting human help to become enormous. Its monetisation strategy based on a vast pool of advertisers fishing in the most appropriate spots is a genius idea for the big players. But although its new junior version, Acast Open, is designed to provide a similar set of opportunities for the bedroom podcasters who may not move much beyond the front room – often happily so – it's no longer free. I put this point to a communications director at Acast for an episode of *How to Grow a Pod*, suggesting that the company that claimed to democratise podcasting has actually created a two-tier system, charging the bedroom heroes while servicing the celebrities for free. She promised to get back to me. She didn't. She was also the only interviewee to fail to send me her audio.

Most podcast hosts will charge a varying rate according to the service they provide. Suzy Buttress of the *Casual Birder* podcast uses the highly popular veteran host Libsyn. 'I have been very happy with the service I get,' she wrote in response to a request for recommendations in the Podcasters' Support Group on Facebook. 'I pay the second tier because I like the additional analytics. I don't like the look of the supplied website and I have a separate website, but all of the distribution is handled by Libsyn.'

Webcomic podcaster Jamais Jochim warned, 'Some sites (such as the free host, Anchor) take on some of the aspects of ownership and make it hard for you to really get into things. I have a guy I'm working with who doesn't give me stats unless I ask for them; that lack of knowledge makes it hard to run a campaign. You're going to have to make compromises. You need to decide on what you're willing to compromise (ownership, price, features) and go for it from there.'

The market is so competitive for podcast hosting that every company will cover the absolute essentials, such as enough storage space for your audio files and sufficient bandwidth for the typical podcaster's needs. PodBean, for example, offers five hours in total, along with a 100 GB monthly bandwidth limit for free, while around £9 per month unlocks the full unlimited package.

All hosts will automatically take care of generating the RSS feed which distributes your podcast to the main directories including Apple Podcasts (iTunes). Depending on which tier you opt for, you will get some details on the performance of your podcast including where in the world your listeners are, how they are listening and where they found you. You may want to know the listening drop-off on your show for example, and this information will cost with some hosts.

Hosts will continue to add to their goodie bags as more and more podcasters come onto the market. Look out for a website for your podcast as standard; if your own website is on WordPress, Blubrry has a free PowerPress plugin which offers a podcasting-optimised WordPress website to its members. Free support should come as standard – some still even offer human support!

Advertising and monetisation options as well as integration tools to grow your pod will increase as hosts compete for better customer service. Podomatic's Pro plan is one of the growing number to offer good revenue options with Patreon and Advertisecast.

Directories

Everyone who wants their podcast listed on iTunes is required to submit it to Apple Podcasts for validation before it appears. You can do this in your settings on any podcast host. You'll need to upload at least two live episodes before you submit to Apple so consider a short trailer and introduction to your podcast if you're not ready to release your first episode. Allow two weeks for this process and don't expect an email confirming validation.

The best way to become discoverable and grow an audience is to list a podcast across every podcast directory; iTunes is not enough. Most good podcasting hosts will automatically list your podcast on Spotify and the major directories, which is an essential part of being found, but you will have to add it manually to Stitcher, Google Podcasts, TuneIn, Castbox, Podcast Addict, iHeartRadio, Overcast and Pocket Casts. Check into the settings of your uploaded podcast and follow the link to add your RSS setting to any one of the directories. You'll receive an email to validate it, but be aware that some hosts – like Acast – will 'obfuscate' your email to avoid unwanted spam. If you're manually signing up for a service like Stitcher, Google Play or Spotify, you may see an email address like info+5dsca7351af@acast.com. You can unmask it by going into the settings on your show, going to Advanced, and toggling the Obfuscate Email button off.

Music

The simple message about using copyright music in podcasting is: *don't*. The complicated laws surrounding music copyright mean that you must use your own, or sign up to a royalty-free music library like Audio Jungle or Audio Blocks (which charges for use and runs a subscription service). The laws are designed to stop anyone depriving artists and publishers of their income, and quite right too. If you really want to use copyright music, head over to Mixcloud, the user-generated internet platform for audio streaming which is fully licensed for copyright music. It partners with many of the largest rights holders, record labels and publishers around the world. It is not distributed via iTunes or Spotify though, which means that your audience is limited.

But don't let that put you off; I won a silver award at the Community Radio Awards in 2016 for my show *Jaibli Salaam*, which was (again) inspired by the idea of Radio 4's *Desert Island Discs*, in which Syrian refugees new to my hometown of Brighton remembered their lives in the old country through their food and favourite music choices. Although it was first broadcast on Radio Reverb, which has a licence to play copyright music, it had to be hosted on Mixcloud to listen again as a podcast. It was the same with *The Write Songs,* another desert island-inspired show which featured the would-be soundtrack to the books of fiction and food writers' books in conversation with their authors. Both were such a joy to produce and a gift to my interviewees that the inevitably low download figures were an irrelevance. I can't even remember when I last looked.

You're almost there. You've got your kit, done your research and signed up for the online forums. But wait, that's just the packaging. If you want to really enjoy podcasting, sit back a while and let me tell you a story . . .

PART II:
Storytelling

9

The Interview

How to tell a story

Whether you're interviewing your hero on the nichest of niche podcasts or working with a huge brand, if you're hoping to compel your listener, you'll need to tell a story. There's no one quite like Ira Glass as storytellers go, so head on to Chapter 10 (p.101) for his masterclass in narrative non-fiction; but first, we go back to the start, pause at the middle and head triumphantly towards the end, gathering some of the best techniques for pulling in your listeners and keeping them with you as you build your community.

So, let's start at the very beginning. Who are you, and who are you talking to? Where are you and why are you talking to this person or these people? What are you talking about? When? These very simple 'W moments' will give shape and clarity to your interview or story. Let's break them down. Let's add another W to the checklist of any journalist and add a W for Weave. Weaving your W moments through an interview will give you a flow and an immersion that takes you well away from your list and your listener into the world that you've created.

The prep

'Hi,' says Pablo in the Facebook Podcasters' Support Group. 'I'm looking for some advice and tips on writing a podcast show script. Does anyone write their show out first? And if so, what is the best software to use? I'm wanting to do a fifteen-minute daily show covering local topics and news, and don't want to wing it.' James Cridland, author of Podnews.net, a must-subscription for podcasters wanting to keep abreast of the latest trends, answered: 'I do a three-minute daily news update about podcasting. It takes about five hours to research and write. Probably ten minutes to edit. I use iA Writer to write the script, but it's also a newsletter and website as well, so you could probably get away with Google Docs or similar.'

I was about to do a remote interview that morning with food writer and 2019 MasterChef champion Irini Tzortzoglou via Zoom with each of us recording locally, Irini on her iPhone using the Voice Memos app and me with my Zoom H4N. As I read Pablo's question, I looked at the four points that I had scribbled in my notebook which would provide the structure of our half-hour chat. I had done my prep; I'd cooked from her beautiful book *Under the Olive Tree* and committed to muscle memory the honey, mustard, oregano, thyme and mint marinade, mixed, of course, with Cretan olive oil and rubbed all over a half shoulder of lamb with garlic and rosemary. I had joked with her about sharing a remote lunch of manouri cheese, pear and grape salad from the book and ate it instead with a friend; the one rule of food podcasting that I've learned is don't eat during an interview! And I had read her book from beginning to end, soaking up the heat of her childhood and dreaming of her food memories. I'd felt the rupture of her story as time and money bound her to banking and left her empty, with no time or inclination to feed herself with the food from home. Her reconnection came through the pain of loss and separation and catapulted her to fame as MasterChef champion, diving deep into her family memories and painting their pictures in a plate of food. I asked her ahead of the interview to email me her four food moments from the book, and it was these that led me through the story of little Irini making trahanas, mixing freshly gathered wheat and soured milk with her tiny fists and laying the results out to dry on the roof of her house, to the 'scraps challenge' on MasterChef when she looked at the various ingredients she had been given and whisked them into a signature dish which told the story of her life. I didn't look at my four points once in the half-hour interview but I still came out with very little to discard.

Everyone has their own process. 'Often with *The Allusionist* I'll go in not having prepared too much,' Helen Zaltzman told me. 'Enough that an interviewee feels respected because they're giving me their time for free, but I want them to feel comfortable and talk freely. Often, I'll have a general idea of what I want, but then afterwards it's about the specific thing they said, and that is the real crux of things.' She lets them speak openly and then narrows it down, honing in on a specific subject or area of conversation. 'I feel like I'm giving them a better experience. I know there are some people that go in with exactly what they want and then they basically wear the interviewee down until they say it. It works for them, but it's not my process at all, partly because it feels like a bit of an ordeal for the interviewee, which I don't want them to go through, given that they're lending me their time for no reason other than generosity; but also, I feel like whatever they have to say is more interesting than the preconceived idea I have of what they could say.'

Hana Walker-Brown's interviews capture the essence of a person in award-winning style and although she creates the immersive experience that has made her one of Britain's most interesting sound designers, it's just her and the Zoom H4N microphone she describes as an extension of her arm. She moves her mic intuitively, and as a yoga teacher with a background in dance, she explained why. 'It's such a technical thing,' she said, referring to audio storytelling, 'recording, and then you're sitting at a computer and that's a very stationary thing when you're editing. And my urge is always to move. So maybe it's just woven in that. I find it very easy to move it around, I suppose, and to have the mic as that extension of me, which means it doesn't get in the way when I'm doing an interview.' The trick to good interviewing is to forget about the microphone, and to enable your interviewee to do so too. 'The sooner they forget the mic,' said Hana, 'the quicker and deeper you can go into someone's story.'

Mic technique

Learning how to use your mic is the key to a successful interview. Hana explained why you need to practise with it first: 'I always say "get to know it" because you need to know when to bring the mic closer, when to pull it down, when to move it further away. It's the cues you're getting off a person in an interview essentially, the body language. If you were comforting someone, maybe you move a little bit closer or if you sense someone needs space, I'll always pull the mic away.'

The Good Stuff with Jenny and the Whale is a podcast from the Church of England's Winchester diocese designed to spread uplifting stories from their parish and the surrounding area. Each episode highlights a story of good work through conversation with the people leading it, with Jenny and John (Whale) taking turns to ask the questions. When I popped over to give them some training after their first couple of episodes, I could tell that they were having issues finding their story, not because they didn't have one, but because it was running away from them even as they were trying to record. Managing an interview is a problem many new podcasters experience, particularly those who don't come from a journalistic background. Undue deference and giving the floor to an interviewee is often the by-product of choosing your stories from a pool of passion projects; the interviewee can be so excited by their subject that you may barely get a word in edgeways. Suddenly that narrative arc of beginning, middle and end is being drawn by someone else, you're feeling flustered and out of your depth and you're about to head home with a couple of hours of audio that you haven't got time to edit.

I taught them how it could be managed with a simple bit of microphone technique. Jenny and John had arrived at their interviewee's home and placed their H4N microphone on the table to record their interview with him and his wife. The four of them sat on each side of the table with John and Jen taking turns to ask their prearranged questions, and often talking over each other as can happen in an informal chat like this. But with the position of mic favouring their main interviewee whose voice and passion for the project were always likely to dominate, the result was a fun, informative, but unwieldy twenty minutes of a listen.

John and Jenny didn't have a handle for their H4N; they had put it flat on the table. Plugging lapel mics or individual mics such as the Rode with its own stand into the machine could have been an option, but Jenny and John had just the basic kit. But the main issue for them was: who's driving the bus?

I showed Jenny and John how picking up the recording device by its handle immediately gave me all the control I needed to take command of the interview, directing it towards myself when I wanted to ask a question and at my interviewee for the answer. A simple shift like this could not only control the interviews throughout the session but enable everyone to be 'on mic', adding a richer, more intimate listen.

Ditching their list of questions which had become incidental and random as the interviewee ran with his story, I asked them to revisit what the initial story was about for them. What had sparked their joy and inspired them to get in touch with their interviewee? Using the W moments – the who/what/when/where/why checklist – I asked them to workshop the story again, and see how many of the answers were in the final piece. With a little more structure driving their questions, the story was able to tell itself.

From the audio, I had no idea where they were recording or where the event that they were discussing took place. I had no picture in my head of it as I was listening, the audio version of a blind spot. The interview felt very static, and I suggested that a tiny addition could make all the difference; recording extra wild track to lay under their introduction could add a sense of place as well as the journey itself. Footsteps on a gravel drive, a car door closing or a doorbell ringing could transform the listening experience and invite the listener into the space with them. John and Jenny are lucky to have Jess, a dedicated editor, on board with their project, and her face lit up as we worked out ways of bringing a straightforward interview up a level with some atmosphere and vox pops from the event itself. With the W moments really focusing in on what the story was and why it had moved Jenny and John enough to want to capture its magic, it quickly became clear how to turn a twenty-minute interview about someone else's passion into a thirty-minute episode that could change the listener's life.

Rob Rosenthal at Transom.org, a showcase and workshop for America's New Public Radio, uses a 'focus sentence': 'Somebody does something because... but...', as Jessica Abel recounts in her fabulous graphic book on storytelling *Out on the Wire*. He explains: the *somebody* is the character in motion, doing *something*. The *because* refers to the motivation for doing it, and *but* presents the challenge. 'In this sentence lies the key to great storytelling,' he tells her.

Ira Glass reminds us to look for the yawn when editing or recording. 'When you're bored is really, really important. It means that something in the story isn't happening in the right way,' he tells Abel in her book. 'What in the story is the bit that you just can't NOT listen to?' Abel says that this is the bit in the story that hints at the 'but' in Rosenthal's focus sentence.

So instead of Jenny and John leaving their microphone passively on the table to capture anything and everything that their interviewee wanted to tell them about his passion project, they could use the W moments to hone into who this person really is and what this passion project has done for his life and for others. Using Rosenthal's focus sentence, they could pull out what they had experienced from the interview in the edit, with a great script framing the story for the listener and shaping it as they dipped in and out of his material to illustrate their points.

The connection

This is when the story starts. Regardless of the rest of the content, the story will be of how you and your interviewee got on. However wonderful your guest is, however compelling the story, if the connection between you and your interviewee makes your listener bored or uncomfortable, they'll switch off.

Once that mic is, as Hana Walker-Brown describes, part of your body, intuitively responding to where the story is at the time, you can begin to listen. Super-listening is the art of great podcasting, but it's not the listener who's doing it but the interviewer. 'The idea of purely listening, not to respond, but listening to actually listen is about holding space for someone else', explained Hana. 'They can be vulnerable.' She thinks that the magic happens when the exchange is acknowledged, 'that you're here to listen, and [the interviewee] is here to tell, and whatever happens beyond that happens later. Right now, it's me and you, and we're just gonna do this. As soon as you offer that and you offer it fully and authentically, that you're not checking your phone or you're not looking at questions on a piece of paper, it's very easy to go very deep into a story.'

A list of questions, pieces of paper, notebooks, are all left outside the room. 'It creates a physical barrier between you and the person,' said Hana. 'What you're trying to do is create this very accelerated intimacy between you and them. I'm not creating moments. I'm not creating feelings that aren't already there. I'm elevating the story. It's about drawing out what already exists and being authentic to the person, to the truth of the story.'

By the time Hana has edited her work, she has removed her voice almost completely. What's left is the essence of that connection between interviewer and interviewee. 'I would argue that I bleed through every single decision,' she told me. 'However you feel listening to it is how I felt in that moment. And that's something I try and bring to every single thing I do.'

Over the next few chapters, we look at how the humble interview is at the heart of great non-fiction storytelling, beginning with the legendary podcasting pioneer, Ira Glass.

POD POINTS

- Remember your W moments – Who? What? When? Where? Why? And Weave
- Do your research
- Master your microphone technique
- Connect with your interviewee

10

The Chicago School of Storytelling

It could be argued that podcasting started with a radio programme. Chicago WBEZ's *This American Life* totally changed the way stories were told on radio when it first hit the airwaves as a weekly show, delivered by Public Radio Exchange in 1995. It created a new style of storytelling that by 1999 the *American Journalism Review* described as 'the vanguard of a journalistic revolution'. With old-school journalism presented as breathtakingly different narrative non-fiction, and each episode a series of 'acts' exploring several subjects linked to a single theme, no one had heard anything like this before. Presenter Ira Glass's introduction to each episode was a thoughtful prologue, his style of intimacy, authority and that dreadful word 'relatability' creating a new narrative voice in radio that resulted in nothing short of an audio revolution.

What followed in America in the 1990s and 2000s, from *Radiolab* to *Invisibilia, StartUp, Reply All, Snap Judgment, Love + Radio* and *Heavyweight,* was built on Glass's and *This American Life's* bricks of narrative journalism. When the same team released *Serial* in 2014 and *S-Town* in 2017, nothing was ever quite the same again.

This American Life (TAL) now has 2.2 million listeners each week across more than five hundred public radio stations in the US, with another 3.1 million people downloading each episode as a podcast. I asked Ira Glass if he saw *This American Life* as radio or podcast. 'It's both,' he told me, 'and for us there's no difference,' he added, referring to the team of thirty or so producers at the *This*

American Life office. 'I mean, I know there are radio shows that don't belong as podcasts, and our radio show predates podcast by years and years, but we're working a format that just happened to adapt very well to the aesthetics of the internet and the aesthetics of podcasting. We just happened to be making a product that happened to be good in this new medium that emerged.'

In a sense *TAL*'s style of storytelling is what radio always was: the nostalgic notion of the family around the radio, listening intently, intimately. Ira agreed: 'In the most traditional sense, somebody's telling you a story,' he told me. 'The way people talk on the show, both in the narration and hopefully in the interviews, has a kind of intimacy to it that's particular to radio, and those things work both as radio and as podcasting.' With headphones cancelling the outside world, the podcast allows the listener to immerse themselves completely. 'The things that make the stories work,' said Ira, 'is that they follow the laws of normal storytelling where we try to pull you in at the beginning with something surprising or interesting, and get you involved in the characters and the situation, and raise questions that then the pod will answer.'

He said it's 'like laying out the beats for a film or a TV series'. Fiction and non-fiction become blurred as the characters and story arcs borrow from classic film storytelling. In episode 126, *Do-Gooders*, Kenny and Jackie Wharton return to retire in their hometown of Canalou, Missouri. As the story of their disastrous community battle is told, *This American Life*-style, it becomes a delicate study of class, social mobility and belonging that could be the subject of a Netflix movie. Glass told me that the team wrestled over the details in the same way as they would an episode of *Serial* or *S-Town*: 'How much do we want to go into this character or this character? How long do we want to linger on this moment?' And in *This American Life*'s particular style, when do you digress? 'You're on this path where you know you're going to start here, you're going to end here,' said Ira. 'And then you want to have moments where you digress for feeling or for funniness or for just weird things that you noticed in the reporting. And so, the question is "How long do you let that spool out?"'

Detail is everything to the *TAL* team. 'We'll have long discussions over things like, wait, in the interview about this guy's life he revealed that he still sleeps with his blanket from when he was a child, even though he's forty-seven. I think that's pretty interesting. Let's go with that for two-and-a-half minutes. But then, can you go with that for two-and-a-half minutes and then come back to the actual story he was there to tell, which was not that?'

Ira and his team have built a lucrative business over the years but have always spent time on their shows. I asked him if podcasters could aspire to its standard without having access to its serious cash. 'We were making these stories before we had money,' he told me. 'I remember my senior producer took a pay cut from her waitress job to come and work for the radio show. And I took a pay cut from my job as a producer for NPR, the American equivalent of the BBC, to start the show. So, we were all working for as little as possible. Like, between \$25–\$40,000. And even the \$40,000 I was making – I was putting ten of it back into the show.' At the beginning, he told me, the staff of four put out forty-eight shows in the first year, not something that he would recommend: 'We were either working or asleep.' He thinks it would be hard 'to gear up to make a weekly show at the scale that we are, because there's just so much material. But I think two people or three people could make a limited series that would be six or eight or ten episodes, twelve episodes, and it could be really special and it would be every bit as good as what we do. The skills that we have are skills that anybody could acquire. To do it every week for years takes a lot of money, but to do it for a one-off doesn't.'

The joy of *This American Life* is the space it gives to a story, the detail, the signposting back to a moment in case we've missed something, the reflection in the moment. This hadn't been heard before in classic radio storytelling, but has since become a feature in long-form narrative non-fiction such as the BBC's *The Missing Cryptoqueen*, the *New York Times*'s *Caliphate* and *The Australian*'s *The Teacher's Pet*. Ira said that the idea is not new. He was inspired early on in his career by a talented interviewer named Noah Adams, a host on an afternoon news show on public radio where he was a young tape cutter. As Ira cut his tape, he listened carefully to how he did it. Like most good interviewers, Adams would stop his interviewee to probe carefully: '"What does that mean, what does that tell you?",' he explained. 'Anybody who is a good interviewer naturally does that. People tell you stories and you say, "Well, what's the point of the story? What does that say?" You know, like interviewing a musician: "What was the music your parents listened to when you were a kid? How did that influence you? What did that do to you?" It's the same structure. It's prod and then idea.' Young Ira would listen to the raw material of Noah Adams, devouring his mentor's interviewing techniques and noticing how he would record much more than he would use, throwing out different theories about what the story would mean as his interviewees told him their tales. 'Half of them wouldn't go anywhere, and half of them would,' said Ira, 'and we would choose the most interesting tape. And that's basically what I do now. When I'm going into an interview, I think *What did this person go through?* And then what might it mean. I think it gives you the most powerful kind of story on the air.'

With the breathiness, the silences and unsteadying rhythm of his narration of *This American Life*, Ira Glass's style has become iconic and much copied. The sound of Glass is the result of super-listening, of imagining so intently what that person in the story was going through that it creates the picture for the listener. 'If they don't have thoughts,' said Ira, 'then suggest thoughts of your own for them to react to.' He told me that it was something that he deliberately developed as an antidote to the 'faux-authority' voice he'd been trained to use as a young reporter at NPR. He remembers one of his colleagues then telling him to notice how 'every time the reporter talked, you'd tune out a little bit, and every time you'd go to a quote from a person you'd tune back in, because the person was just talking like a person. And that's what a good presenter does. They sound relaxed and good, even if they're speaking in a kind of performed way. I want to try to get my narration to sound more like I really talk.'

He admits that it took practice: 'I consciously wanted to retrain myself and how I sounded on the air. We started a little local show that was on late night Friday night and Chicago radio only, that we called *The Wild Room*. And then, what I would do is bring in scripts and quotes and music and perform it live.' He practised this way for five years before he started *This American Life*. 'It was just trying to invent a different sound. The fact that it's been imitated is really one of the most surprising things that's happened to me. I don't think of it as like a style of broadcasting, I just think of it as *this is how I talk*.'

It's a legacy that everyone in narrative non-fiction is happy to attribute to Ira Glass and he is a legend in podcasting. In the next chapter, we'll meet some of the radio producers who have followed his lead, taking the Chicago sound to the heart of British broad- and podcasting.

TECH talk

Microphones

Ira Glass says, 'I like the AT8035 Audio Technica shotgun. A shotgun is better for everything: quieter interviews because less room noise, better in scene tape because you can point it where you want it.'

Recorders

'Lots of recorders are good. I use the 4-Track Zoom. Transom.org is the best place evaluating audio gear for this kind of work. [They offer a] wonderful rundown of software, hardware, mics – everything – plus tips on how to use it well.'

Editing software

'I like Pro Tools but there are so many good ones. Descript is the one so many people are excited about now: it transcribes and then you edit the transcript and it moves the audio around.'

<<<Listen to Ira Glass on How to Grow a Pod. *>>>*

11

Podcast to Pictures

When BBC radio producer Georgia Catt and her boyfriend went to the pub with their mates one evening two years ago, she had no idea that she would come away with an idea for a podcast that would set new standards in British audio storytelling, hit 4.7 million downloads in the first six months and sell to the highest bidder at a TV auction.

Georgia is one of the producers of Radio 4's *The Untold*, a series which echoes the immersive storytelling championed by Ira Glass and the team at *This American Life*. With host Grace Dent whispering in our ears, signposting moments we might otherwise miss, everyday dramas behind the curtains of normal life become compelling tales and essential listening. But it was *The Missing Cryptoqueen* which took that format and raised it, with a story that was so unlikely that it had to be true.

Back to the pub. Georgia told me how her friend introduced her to the story of OneCoin. 'He got out his phone and started telling me about a new investment that he'd made,' she said. 'There was a dial in a screen on his phone and it showed that his investment – something like €7000 – had already reached €38,000 in this new cryptocurrency. And he said that in the next six months, it was going to triple that. He was like, "It's gonna go up and up and up."'

Spotting the story

Maybe it takes a producer's brain to see the potential for a story right from the get-go, but it was a goosebumps moment for Georgia. She had heard of Bitcoin but this, her friend told her, was going to democratise cryptocurrency. A story about to unravel that no one else is talking about? That's worth a Google. 'I remember sitting there,' she said, 'and I don't know a huge amount about crypto-currency, but what I did know is that my friends who have invested in things like Bitcoin can take their money out if they want. They can buy things with that Bitcoin, whereas the money on this person's account was just stuck there on the screen.' His enthusiasm, the potential reward and the fact that she had never heard of it piqued her interest. She went home and began to investigate. 'My boyfriend and I must have spent three or four months just obsessing over this, going down the rabbit hole,' she told me.

She found Facebook pages, 'mad' websites and 'incredible' videos of the founder of OneCoin, Dr Ruja Ignatova, a captivating Romanian woman, always dressed in expensive ball gown, long diamond earrings and bright red lipstick, presenting to thousands on stage in huge arenas against a backdrop of anthemic music, pyrotechnics and glitter. 'She was like a Messiah,' said Georgia. 'She was promising a new financial revolution, and I just couldn't get enough of it.'

But it was only when Georgia started engaging with people in the online groups that she realised that this was a world that most people didn't know about. 'I think it's sort of fallen down the cracks between mainstream media and those who found it a bit niche and weird.' She had wanted to do something about cryptocurrency for some time, 'I think because it's a real, quite defined world. You're either in it or you're not. And if you're in it, you are often absolutely evangelical about it.'

And then, as she was doing her preliminary investigations, Dr Ruja Ignatova disappeared off the face of the earth, leaving millions of her fans wondering about the future of their investments. There was no explanation. no one was talking. Could she have been murdered? Could she have changed her identity as her plan spun out of control? Suicide? There it was: the cliff hanger essential to every gripping storyline. Suddenly, Georgia's idea for a bizarre single documentary had become a true crime story which could unfold in real time.

The pitch

She pitched it to the BBC Radio Documentary & Specialist Factual Unit, the home of single documentaries and series, including *Short Cuts* and *The Untold* where she is a producer. 'I didn't really mind where it went as long as it had space to get in-depth,' she said. 'Because the other amazing thing about this story was that it's not just a missing woman. It's this world that taps into so many things going on now, whether it's distrust in the mainstream media and the banking systems, whether it's fake news, how easy it is to construct credibility online.'

And podcasting is the medium for the deep dive. Her boss saw its potential as a long-running series, and they took it to BBC Sounds where the podcast format can offer the elasticity to develop a much more nuanced series. 'I knew I wanted to have a decent space to investigate it properly,' she told me. 'BBC Sounds was quite new at that stage and we had a meeting with the commissioning editor and I suggested it and he ran with it.' With technology journalist Jamie Bartlett on board as presenter, she had the first green light for her show.

But the commissioning process was more challenging as the longer-form narrative requires a bigger budget and therefore a suitably rigorous proposal. 'They wanted a really in-depth breakdown of what the episodes could sound like,' said Georgia, who found the drilling down and mapping out a useful experience. 'I think that was really important. You need to know that it's good if you're going to commit to eight episodes. You need to know that there's going to be enough in there. But I remember writing this and thinking, *There's more. There's no problem because it does open up these worlds.* But when we were initially structuring it, I wanted the chase for Dr Ruja to be central.'

The structure

The plan was for each episode to wander into different territories as Jamie and Georgia hunted down the missing cryptoqueen, bumping into bizarre worlds and heading down their rabbit holes: the Miss OneCoin beauty pageant in Romania, the Amsterdam billionaire network marketeer, the money laundering . . . And as they found themselves in hot water, so did we. The episodes were being released as Jamie and Georgia were still on the road playing their own game of Grandmother's Footsteps, even as news of their search for Dr Ruja was reaching OneCoin's inner circle. And they did *not* like the BBC. As they took to Twitter to trash their claims, the listeners were part of the story. *We* felt chased, hunted and shut down as much as Jamie and Georgia were. As they found themselves at the OneCoin beauty pageant, despite the comic value, we felt the menace. 'Jamie's done some pretty weird stuff,' Georgia told me. 'He's hanging out with those sorts of fringe groups all the time. And he said, "This is possibly the most uncomfortable I've ever felt."'

The Teacher's Pet podcast – the eight-part investigation by journalist Hedley Thomas and *The Australian* newspaper into the cold case of wife and mother Lynette Dawson, who went missing in the early eighties – used the same format and even led to the arrest of Dawson's husband thirty years on. Releasing episodes as the investigation was still ongoing meant that Hedley could feed responses into the narrative as new witnesses lined up to tell their part of the story. Georgia hadn't quite planned to be as reactive as she had to be. 'When it was commissioned, my thought was that by then the company would have collapsed. There's too much scrutiny on it.

And, I mean, it wasn't just going; it was fighting back against what we were saying. And so we really built in what was happening as we were investigating.'

And the joy was that you didn't need to know about any of these to follow the plot. Tech-nerd Jamie even rings his mum at one point to check she understands a bit of the script which describes cryptocurrency. She doesn't. He goes back to the drawing board. It's *This American Life* UK-style. 'I think podcasts totally allow you to do that,' said Georgia. 'They allow you to do that so long as the listener trusts in the hosts – the journalists – as long as this isn't manipulative, that there is a purpose to it. As long as it doesn't sound like filler. I really hope that wasn't the case with us.'

You can hear the whole story of how Georgia and Jamie put *The Missing Cryptoqueen* together on *How to Grow a Pod,* but I asked her how much she had been inspired by the Ira Glass school of storytelling as she began to sculpt the show. 'I think that he and *This American Life* have done so much for narrative storytelling and increasing the interest in it as well,' she said. 'I think one of the big things that first drew me to those stories and kept me listening was how he [Ira] wasn't the traditional top-down host. He was absolutely engaged with the story himself. There's something about seeing it in almost a cinematic way and how you structure it; it's not a kind of clip link, clip link—' referring to the classic news format of audio reportage or interview followed by narrator/reporter explanation. 'It is how you leave the audience wanting more.'

The legacy of *TAL* is the format, the pure *style* of its narrative non-fiction and it is one that amateurs can and do copy. But Georgia is not alone in pointing out how much more money is spent on the shows. Ira Glass says in Chapter 10 that it wasn't always so, but Georgia's BBC Sounds budget was shoestring, and amateurs may find themselves crowdfunding or applying for grants to help them realise their dreams. 'I absolutely love *This American Life,*' said Georgia, 'and

I think what they've done is fantastic. But I'm always amazed when I listen to the end credits, and the amount of people that they have working on one of these programmes, especially one of their big series like *Serial* or *S-Town*. I can count the people on one hand who were involved in *The Missing Cryptoqueen*.'

The plot

The podcast is the perfect platform for such a story: one that twists and turns, pops off on a tangent and comes back with a cliff hanger to make your jaw drop. It's the Netflix phenomenon, the boxset binge that allows for total immersion in a story, and long car journeys will never be the same again. The mix of interviews and witness actuality, including emergency service phone calls and police testimonies, set against well-written narration by talented journalists, has become one of the most successful genres in podcasting. *The Teacher's Pet* was downloaded 50 million times in its first year. *Dirty John*, an eight-part series following misadventures in online love by Christopher Goffard of the *LA Times* led to a Netflix series, as did *Fake Heiress*, the six-parter by journalist Vicky Baker and playwright Chloe Moss which explored the scandal of Anna Delvey, the New York conwoman who duped the city's high society into believing that she was a multi-millionaire heiress.

And we may be seeing a rise in narrative non-fiction as brands and advertising agencies recognise the influence of the podcast and its potential. Josh Adley, director of communications at podcasting production company Listen, told me that the phenomenon is the result of *Serial*. 'That was a ground-breaking moment when I realised that a lot of my friends who have never listened to a podcast before started to take interest. Clearly that has gone on to be one of the most – if not *the* most – successful podcasts of all time and made true crime one of the most popular genres within podcasting. You can see companies like Wondery (which co-produced *Dirty John* with the *LA*

Times) who are making an impressive array of shows within that genre.'

It's a big ask to expect people to listen to eight hours of storytelling, especially in one sitting, but also to keep coming back for more. But Josh believes that *Serial* has shown that there is unlimited potential for storytelling in podcasting. 'People are on their commute to and from work, or out for a walk, or at the gym, or cooking. It's that opportunity to distract your mind. I think that over the past few years, people have become even busier than they were and potentially more time-poor, and a podcast is a great opportunity to fill that gap.'

Podcasting and the commercial

It's such a clear market that Wise Buddha, the twenty-five-year-old radio production company, launched its own podcasting arm, Listen, to focus specifically on this emerging medium for storytelling. 'We realised that we were starting to see a massive uplift in our work in podcasting,' said Josh, 'and the radio opportunities weren't increasing at the same rate. You can count the slots available for storytelling in BBC and commercial radio on one hand, and podcasting became the key focus for us. We are making more money from our podcast than we are radio and we are seeing all of our new business opportunities coming in podcasting. It's now absolutely the core focus of our business. We made that transition so that people saw us as a podcast company and not a radio company.'

Josh comes from an advertising background and looks for ways of matching brands to what people want to listen to. BBC Sounds is the podcasting unit of the BBC and, according to the BBC Charter, cannot accept sponsorship or advertising, leaving the drama and narrative non-fiction market open to monetisation as an increasing number of professional storytellers and writers turn to podcasting to try out their ideas for film and TV.

Audio drama production company Sweet Talk is already making

fiction podcasts for Radio 4 and BBC Sounds, and producer/director Karen Rose told me that the difference between radio drama and podcasts is noticeable. 'It's early days but the main difference lies in the need to make your podcast marketable since it doesn't have a guaranteed audience, unlike with radio plays. Casting a star isn't enough. The upside is that podcast listeners are mostly on earbuds so there's an active engagement as opposed to radio listeners who may only have the play on in the background.'

It's *Serial* again that provides the context. 'At the moment the form veers towards storytelling with a narrator partly because it's easier to write,' she told me. 'When there are no visual cues, writing exposition which doesn't sound clunky is a real challenge. But also because the listeners have moved across from factual storytelling like *Serial* so they are more engaged with the intimacy of a one-to-one with a host.'

Sweet Talk adapted the works of vintage American horror writer H. P. Lovecraft, who already has a solid online following, into a fictional mystery podcast, one of the most successful genres for keeping listeners engaged across multiple episodes. Mystery, thriller and supernatural genres tend to attract younger listeners too, and often the more discerning listener, according to Karen: 'Those who are really into sound, like the gamers who love the immersive, filmic soundscapes underscored with music. It's often recorded on location with the mic following the action rather than something that is created in the studio.' As I write, she and the crew are recreating Beirut in the woods behind my house, using the skills of her sound engineer and the imagination of her director to turn rural Sussex into a war zone. She's enjoying the freedom of not being tied to a specific length. And there are other benefits: 'We can say fuck and everything!' she laughed.

The current feeding frenzy for long-form storytelling is good news for all audio storytellers as the increase in quality attracts new audiences hungry for content. Once a medium for a younger demographic, podcasting is now pulling in listeners of all ages, many migrating seamlessly from Radio 4 via BBC Sounds and looking for other podcasts to listen to once they have binged on a series. Georgia Catt told me that she finds the line is often blurred between radio and podcast. 'I listened to *Girl Taken* on Radio 4 the other day, and it was an amazing story about a guy who tried to bring a small child from Canada over to England. I just think you need the ability to go in depth and to have one episode that's an hour and one that's twenty-five minutes, depending on what it's worth. That's the key difference between radio and podcast.'

It's already happening on BBC Sounds and Audible. 'You're seeing brilliant podcasts and series coming through,' said Georgia, 'Stories that combine really good original investigation and journalism with the best in storytelling. What I do starts with a small story that just gets bigger and bigger and bigger as it spirals out. But you should never try and be like something else. You just have to look out for these great stories and run with them. When you find them, be yourself. Be creative with it.'

How does an amateur find a good story? Well, usually it will find you. It'll be the 'aha' moment that makes the hairs stand up on the back of your neck, the time when you lean in and ask *'really?'* It tends to be lurking in the quirky, nerdy, ordinary tales of everyday life, often with a subtle signpost to the extraordinary twist that makes your jaw drop. The trick is to spot the twist before anyone else does. As with *This American Life*, it's usually the small-town stuff that tells the biggest stories, the local newspaper reports that, with a little prod, open to reveal something that deep down we all know. Georgia says that it's time consuming to turn them into the kind of stories that we love, that it's hard work and, on a BBC salary, not a great money-earner, but for her it's worth every minute. 'I just hope there's more of them,' she says. 'They're all challenges we can meet, I'm sure.'

The storytellers, investigative reporters and drama producers among you who are considering testing out your Big Idea in a podcast will know how much work you need to do to create something of the standard of the podcasts discussed here. But as the market opens up and the money flows, it may well be worth it. As the audience expands and sponsors smack their lips at the number and variety of scripts piling into their inbox, podcasting is a very real option to the growing number of platforms for storytelling.

Research is key to understanding what time and space can offer a podcast, and also when they can hamper it. For all the extraordinary outcomes of the flabby *Teacher's Pet* (no spoilers here), wading through its seventeen episodes of between 50 and 120 minutes each had me begging for an editor. We may well have stretched our notion of time with Netflix and now podcasting, but any story still needs to hold our attention throughout, shifting gear and keeping up the surprises as it careers towards its denouement.

POD POINTS

- Find the extraordinary in the ordinary
- Research!
- Keep the story tight
- Podcast drama is *hot* right now

12

The Producers

The humble interview may be at the heart of any great storytelling, but it's also something of an art. In this chapter, we meet some of the professional producers who are raising the game in DIY podcasting by bringing their old-media skills to this plucky new platform.

Alison Vernon-Smith has thirty years' experience as a producer in broadcasting at the BBC and in the independent sector. Since leaving the BBC, she produces high-end, sponsored podcast series for brands, such as Harrods' *True Tales of Luxury* presented by Mariella Frostrup and Belstaff's *The Road Less Travelled* with Reggie Yates. She was the first podcast producer I knew to put a proper price on her head. While the rest of us were taking what we could get, Alison was asking for what she was due, and the market responded. She is now one of many professional podcast producers who can shine up a podcast idea and make it attractive to a suitable sponsor or one of the many new commissioners such as Spotify, Audible and BBC Sounds.

She brings old-school BBC standards to a world which has been defined by difference and innovation but which can often sound amateur. Increasingly, brands that spot the potential in podcasting are coming into the marketplace and, despite its punky rep, still prefer what they see as a safe pair of hands. Alison's style of producing is an antidote to the DIY ramble beloved of so many podcasters and podcast fans but is useful for anyone working with interviewees, if only to learn the rules before breaking them. 'Because I'm very BBC,' she told me, 'it took me a long time to get used to the sound of podcasts. I still don't like lots of them because I just think, *Oh, for God's sake, stop waffling. Who edited this? And why am I listening to this person? Why is it taking you five minutes to say what could be said in twenty seconds?* And I still quite like *tight*. Unless they're really interesting people – and there's very few of those to be honest – they do need editing. They need a presenter who's going to whip them into shape and get it out of them more quickly. That's what a producer does.'

It's what *BBC* producers do, but podcasting can often benefit from a looser grip, a well-prepared record-as-live show in which whatever happens makes for the kind of relaxed listen that an audience often expects from a podcast. *That Peter Crouch Podcast*, for example, may have baffled Radio 4 listeners according to its *Feedback* show with its banter and schoolboy humour, but it consistently tops the podcast charts.

For most podcasters, it's not even a question; the budget simply doesn't allow for a producer. But it's also because it's *their* show. They don't want to be told what to do. One of the real joys of hobbyist podcasting is making up your own rules and monetising your show yourself – if at all. But it probably won't be commissioned by Audible or Spotify.

Alison's first show for Spotify, *We Need to Talk About . . .*, was honed from her experience producing Radio 4's *Midweek* in which four guests would join a round-table to discuss their latest work. Intersections were carefully orchestrated with the help of a script carved from research and briefing notes on each guest. 'Spotify had commissioned this production company to produce a weekly topical show with [TV presenter] Jolyon Rubinstein,' she told me. 'They wanted Jolyon and so it was our job to come up with a format. It was basically a round-table discussion programme so, as an exec, it was my job to decide on tone, calibre of guest and how to work with Jolyon who had never done this before.'

She explained that the host needs to be able to orchestrate a discussion between people, 'to make sure that the people who you've got on as guests all get a fair crack at the whip'. Keeping guests happy by ensuring that their side of the deal is met, usually plugging their book or tour early on in the programme, makes for a relaxed atmosphere and an easy listen, but it also builds an important relationship with the show. A happy guest (and publicist) is more likely to share the show on social media but may also come back and open the door to their celebrity or niche-interest friends.

Professional presenters are used to working with producers and although, as Mariella Frostrup does, they may absorb their briefing notes and then perfect their own scripts, they are often happy to be guided by the producer. 'I've always approached the [shows] as I would a BBC programme,' said Alison. 'So the same amount of work goes into them as it would if it was on Radio 4.' She says her clients and her presenters expect that level of professionalism from her; 'They want to make the best that they can,' she said. 'They're not shy of asking for help or for advice, and they have a much more collaborative relationship with a producer. The only people who push back on it are, to my mind, people who are a bit insecure and who have not done it very much.'

The podcasting world is now a sea of opportunity, but I asked Alison if she thought there was room for the ocean-going liners produced by former BBC producers *and* the amateur shows produced by hobbyists bobbing around in the shallows. 'There's room for all sorts of things,' she told me, 'but if I'm going to listen to a round-table discussion, I want clever people saying interesting things that mean something. I don't want to listen to twenty minutes of boredom to get to two interesting points.'

She suggests that you should do what you're good at. 'If you're going to try and replicate something that's been done by a professional producer and you've spent a few hours editing it, it's not going to sound the same, and if it's badly recorded . . . So, don't do that would be my advice. Do something completely different. If you do a podcast about birdwatching for example, don't sit in the studio talking about it; take me out and show me the birds and listen to the birds. That would be completely different. In audio I think passion is the most important thing, beyond anything else. Somebody who is a good storyteller, who is passionate about what they're talking about, you can't beat that. So, if you haven't got lots of facility and you're a very slow editor – and to be honest editing is just practice – then do something that doesn't require it to sound professional and polished, because it's not going to be that.'

Authorship and opinion is the territory of the podcast, a place where conversation is a bit looser, a little more meandering and time is determined by what feels right, although there's a generally accepted notion of the sweet spot being about thirty minutes. 'You get a lot more of the presenter in a podcast,' said Alison. 'The host is going to tell you what they think. I don't want to know what [BBC TV and radio presenter] Andrew Marr thinks about things. He might add a comment or two in *Start the Week*, for example, but you're not interested in what Andrew Marr thinks about. He's not an expert.' Compare the behaviour of BBC correspondents Chris Mason and Laura Kuenssberg, who were barely off our screens and smart speakers throughout the three long, drawn-out years of Brexit, and their performances on BBC Sounds' *Brexitcast*. In the latter, it sounded as if they could loosen their ties, kick off their shoes and have a laugh while they gave us the back story to their week in politics. It's a clever move by the BBC; it feels like we've been invited to the after-party while reinforcing and deepening our connection with its star presenters.

But it's not just the BBC that encourages its talent to present a more chilled version of themselves in their podcasts. Matt Hill produces Fearne Cotton's *Happy Place* podcast and explained to me why she wanted to do her own thing. He described how her personality is divided between the podcast and her BBC Radio 2 show. 'Her more authentic self is allowable on her own podcast,' he told me. 'It feels like she owns that space, that she can do whatever she wants to do with it.' Actually, she really does own that space, but Matt says that her investment is much more than financial. 'She is the one booking the guests,' he told me. 'That's part of a process that she *should* own, because it comes across in the episodes. Some of her standout episodes, the ones she's most proud of, are ones where she starts, "I've been trying to get this person on the show for months now," or years. Elizabeth Gilbert is a huge hero of hers and that really comes across in the intro to that show. I think the one with Hillary Clinton, which is a massive coup, was a lot of hard work on her part. And that really comes across, and it gives it a kind of authenticity.'

Perhaps it's because Matt is more hands-off with Fearne's podcast than Alison is with her professional presenters that *Happy Place* sounds like it really is the place that makes Fearne smile. Matt says his main job is to listen. 'My role begins once the guest is booked and we've met for the interview,' he told me. 'Fearne will book the guests and write the questions and set the agenda. And then, once we get into the recording – which I'll be setting up whether that's on location face-to-face, booking a studio or doing it remotely – once we've set up and got the best quality sound we can, what I'll be doing is listening to that interview as Fearne does it.' Of course, she is a consummate live presenter: 'She knows how to do the work on the tempo and the peaks and troughs and make it all work, so I leave that bit to her. I give her a bit of timings as we go through, just to make sure she knows when we need to wrap up.' Matt then 'tidies up' by filling in any gaps. As a second pair of ears, he listens on behalf of the listener and makes notes throughout the recording before asking Fearne to do 'pick ups', anything that she might have missed in the moment. 'It's to make sense of something that didn't quite make sense at the time,' said Matt. For most podcasters who can't afford a producer, this is known as the 'damn it' moment, usually in the edit when it's too late to go back!

Solo podcasters have to do the job of producer, presenter and editor, listening intently to their guests, making sure that they're getting what they need for the interview but also that their listener's needs are being met. This has to happen in the moment and can be tricky; when I was recording an interview for *Cooking the Books* with Joanne Harris about her latest book in the *Chocolat* series, *The Strawberry Thief*, I was aware that she was a little prickly with me. I suspected that it was because I had made an assumption in my opening preamble that the arrival of Vianne and little Anouk in their red cloaks, an iconic moment in a scene from the film of *Chocolat,* had come from the book. I had seen the film very recently but hadn't read the book in years. It wasn't. Joanne was polite but frosty and clearly thought that I was an idiot. I thought quickly about whether I'd edit that out later – we were, after all, talking about *The Strawberry Thief* rather than *Chocolat*. But I also had to work out whether my discomfort was compelling or just downright uncomfortable for the listener, and what to do about it. My inner fangirl won the vote and I *made* her like me, using examples from her work to show just how much I'd noticed about her writing process, how deeply I'd understood what she was really trying to say, taking my listener with me through the nettles to a cosy mug of hot chocolate of a listen. Joanne Harris had put me on the back foot by not liking me (How could that be? I was her biggest fan! This was my biggest coup to date. Roll over Nigella and Ottolenghi, this was my moment.) I think I won. And perhaps it was because I had to fight hard for my trophy that the episode is one of the most popular in Series 1 of *Cooking the Books*. Had I flagged it up in the introduction, I might have pulled the listener in with me even earlier.

It's this authenticity, an unplanned moment or a deliberate move to loosen your stays, that is podcasting gold and can be found in the best podcasts, from the smallest to the biggest shows. Your favourite podcaster feels like your best friend, someone who is in your life, in your *head* every single week. It's a direct bond with a single listener. Miranda Sawyer wrote in the *Observer* that we don't even like to share our very favourite podcasts, so intimate is our relationship with them.

So how can a Radio 4, Radio 1, 6 Music or 5 Live show also be a podcast? If a more relaxed, cooler style is the podcast look, how can the sharper, suited and booted BBC sound also be called a podcast? Is it simply about the accessibility? Alison Vernon-Smith told me how as an executive producer in comedy at Radio 4, she was encouraged to commission ideas that could be downloaded, a platform which had huge advantages. 'The BBC comedy programmes got huge, huge download figures, and still do.' It was a stroke of genius, a way of creating long-life programmes on a BBC (read: relatively small) budget. But the influence of podcasting, certainly *This American Life*-style podcasting, was heading down the corridors of New Broadcasting House and into the offices of non-narrative fiction. *Short Cuts* and *The Untold* gave birth to multi-episodic meandering yarns like *The Missing Cryptoqueen*, which could only have been made as a podcast with its eleven hour-long episodes, and *Fake Heiress*, the Radio 4 series released indefinitely on Sounds. With newspapers like the *LA Times* producing long-form shows like *Dirty John*, with original material from 911 calls cleverly reworked to create compelling storytelling out of reportage, and independent production companies signing up to the Equality in Audio Pact, which assures payment for interns, the future is bright for multi-platform journalists in the comparatively low budget world of podcasting.

In the same way as Netflix has changed the structure of drama and of non-fiction storytelling with the boxset binge, podcasting too encourages the listener to settle in for the long haul, slowing down the action and enabling more of the back story to be revealed. Alison

Vernon-Smith is excited about the future but warns against copycat podcasting which will never be as good as the original. 'I think [BBC's 2019 podcast] *Tunnel 29* is really good, but I find it really derivative of Ira Glass's work in *Serial* and *S-Town*, which are brilliantly produced. However, I have to say, if you listen to the list of credits at the end of *Serial* and *S-Town*, I couldn't believe how many people are involved in that. They've got script editors coming out of their ears! That's just not possible in the BBC. You haven't got the money for that.'

With an increasing number of professional teams – made up of executive producer, producer and presenter – vying for the podcast audience's attention, being the best you can be is important. For those having a lovely time bobbing along on the waves, podcasting as a passion project and often earning very little if anything at all, what chance do they have to stay afloat? I asked Alison how you can tell whether your podcast is any good if you made it without someone to bounce ideas off. 'Well, I suppose if lots of people download it and listen to it, then it must be quite good. If you're working with a presenter, [they] will say, "That's a bit shit, isn't it?" Or, "Let's not do that, let's do something else." I suppose you would know that it wasn't completely shit, but you'd always be a bit worried that it was and you just hadn't clocked it.'

And there it is. The democracy of the podcasting world. If it's good enough, the people will listen. And it's why, as Jason Allan Scott tells us in Chapter 15 (p.147), the average podcaster completes between three and five episodes before giving up. But if you've got a bit of spare cash, you care enough about awards, you're staking or building a professional reputation on your work or you're looking for sponsorship or advertising revenue, you could hire a freelance producer to critique your podcast for around £200 for half a day's work.

I asked Alison to listen to the episode in Season 1 of *Cooking the Books* which features my interview with food writer Jeff Gordinier on his road trip with one of the world's greatest chefs, René Redzepi, for his book *Hunger*. I explained to her that *Cooking the Books* is a series for foodies who love to read about food. It's deliberately niche and offers high quality interviews with famous food writers, usually about their latest books. I am fairly well known in the food community, particularly because of my work with the *delicious.* podcast. *delicious.* magazine is a highly respected food magazine in the UK, and I have interviewed most of the writers, chefs, producers and personalities in this small pond.

Alison's main criticism of the episode was the introduction; she said that while the episode was enjoyable to listen to, she wasn't told what it was about or told enough about Jeff or René Redzepi to understand why she should continue to listen. The old adage for public speaking, 'Tell 'em what you're going to say, then tell 'em, then tell 'em what you've just said', is just as appropriate for any kind of storytelling, and podcasting is no exception. 'On the whole,' wrote Alison, 'I think a show needs to hook its audience right at the start. So how are you going to do this? It's got to be intriguing or emotional, or it's got to tell me very early doors why I might want to spend the next few minutes with you. And then make me want to carry on listening. It's got to sustain my interest until it's over.'

Here's the original introduction to the episode:

- Welcome to *Cooking the Books* with me, Gilly Smith, the podcast for foodie book lovers where food is the story, and this month, it's sponsored by City Books, Brighton and Hove's largest and liveliest independent bookshop.
- This week, by the magic of Zoom, I'm in Manhattan in the home of former *New York Times* journalist and author of *Hungry*, Jeff Gordinier, to retrace the footsteps of what must be one of the best

food journalist gigs ever, a rock 'n'roll road trip with René Redzepi, the greatest chef in the world.

–   In the week that Redzepi re-opens the doors at Noma, his Copenhagen restaurant which has been voted the best restaurant in the world no less than four times, Jeff has a good guess at what this pioneer of the new Nordic locavore movement and master of reinvention is going to do with the latest incarnation of Noma, an outdoor-only $15-a- burger-and-wine bar. But first, I asked him about the moment he was offered the opportunity to go to Mexico with René Redzepi.

Alison explained how a few tweaks could lift this and invite listeners in. 'There are a lot of ways of starting this,' she suggested in her report, 'a clip from the book, a clip of the interview, some startling facts about the protagonists, a news clip of the restaurant or something about the chef.' She took me through the standard format for an introduction:

1.   What is this podcast ... (peak music)
2.   This week I'm talking to ... (little clip of guest)
3.   Explain who bloke is and what he's talking about ...

Take two:

–   Welcome to *Cooking the Books* with me, Gilly Smith, the podcast for foodie book lovers where food is the story and this month, it's sponsored by City Books, Brighton and Hove's largest and liveliest independent bookshop. Each week I take a food writer through the four moments in their book that add a little depth and flavour to their memoir or cookbook, or put the meat on the bones of their biography. [PEAK MUSIC]
–   This week, by the magic of Zoom, I'm in Manhattan in the home of

food editor at American *Esquire*, Jeff Gordinier. As he takes me through his four food moments in his book *Hungry*, we retrace the footsteps of what must be one of the best food journalist gigs ever, a rock 'n' roll road trip with René Redzepi, the greatest chef in the world

– [CLIP:] There's a bit of the cult leader about him [laughter]. And basically he said, 'You and I are going to go to Mexico – it's my favourite place in the world – and we're going to feast and explore life,' and I'm like, Wait, we've just met. Why? What is happening? [laughter]

– In the week that Redzepi re-opens the doors at Noma, his $200-a-head Copenhagen restaurant, which has been voted the best restaurant in the world no less than four times, Jeff introduces us to the genius, the gentleman and the giant of the Nordic locavore movement and tells me what he thinks he'll do with his new $15-a-burger-and-wine bar.

– But first, I asked him about the moment he was offered the opportunity to go to Mexico with René Redzepi.

Who knows if it was Alison's intro structure that I applied in Season 2 that helped the sudden growth in the audience? Granted, I went back to my *delicious.* podcast heartland in Season 2 with guests only from food writing, which I know so much better than the much broader world of fiction, but I like to think that the more confident tone which comes from constructive criticism might have gone some way in winning me some of my new listeners.

Podcasting is usually a solitary activity, and I'd be lying if I said that I haven't enjoyed working with the editorial teams on my branded podcasts. Chris Little, one of the two producers of Leon's *How to Eat to Save the Planet* gave me the perfect blend of positive feedback and constructive criticism to help me understand exactly what he wanted from the podcast and the all-important confidence to push my skills and ideas up a level. As a former TV producer, he understands story. 'Those little food miles nuggets are so good and lift the piece into something more widely informative,' he emailed me about the first episode I recorded for them about a hyper-local gourmet restaurant in Brighton. 'And the way the Isaac At interview complements it works beautifully. Dom really liked the sous vide element so well done for sticking to your guns on that one! We're both agreed that the music still isn't quite right but that's on us to figure out what music we want on this and all our other content.' I knew what he wanted from the rest of the series. The sheer energy in his response was a joy: 'Just listening to [the] salmon [episode].' I could see him tapping his thoughts on WhatsApp, headphones still in. 'The intro is perfection. Music works beautifully and the way it moves into their initial quotes is perfect. Nailed it.'

As your granny would tell you, there's no 'I' in team, and it was good to feel part of something bigger. But there is also a freedom in *not* being produced, in finding your own way and doing it yourself, from booking the guests to working up the format and the sponsorship, even if it can get exhausting. With *Cooking the Books*, which I produce and present myself, I've discovered a voice that I didn't have at Leon or at *delicious.* and it's *mine*. I've realised my own value by taking the time to discover what makes me unique in food podcasting. And that gives me the leverage for any number of new opportunities.

POD POINTS

- Keep your content tight
- Get a second opinion
- If you don't want to use a producer, *think* like one

13

The Editors

The story is only half of what it takes to tell a tale. As Ira Glass tells us, the time spent on the edit is where the art is.

Without the distractions of location or the frisson of the rapport, the edit is an intense opportunity to hear what really happened when you were out recording. Listen to the sound of silence. What does it say to you? No longer just the interviewer now, you're the one who makes a judgement as a listener. Does it make you prick up your ears, sense an unguarded moment? Does it make you uncomfortable? If so, is that a good thing? Can you cope when the interviewee stops talking? As an editor, what can you learn about your interview technique? What do you hear when *you* stop talking? Have you dried up or are you making a point? Perhaps leaving a void to be filled? Are you manipulating or allowing? Forcing or enabling? As an editor, what do you do with those silences?

The joy of the podcast is that this is where you learn the most. Whatever you've got at source can be restructured in the edit, layered with atmosphere, music, effects and any number of fancy moves in post-production to make a very different-sounding story. A voiceover can give a different take on the story, or it can ensure that an emphasis or bias is clear. I asked Matt Hill, Fearne Cotton and Olly Mann's producer and co-founder and judge of the British Podcast Awards, about the moment where he thinks, *That's got to go.* 'Well, for me I think the editorial choice is leaving things in,' he said. I asked him about ums and ers in particular, a popular question in the Facebook forums. 'In,' he told me. 'You're making a point of saying that they didn't know the answer to that, or that they had to think for a long time about it.'

What about silence? 'The grammar of audio is that, even though people don't necessarily understand the terminology behind it, listeners will gravitate towards a silence and wonder what's coming next, what they're thinking about, what they don't want to think about, what they don't want to talk about,' said Matt. 'For the shows that I do where there's nothing to hide, we make a really clear point of saying, "We're not actually trying to screw anyone over here, this isn't meant to be *gotcha* journalism; we want to have an honest conversation, we want you to be open about that, and so we're going to provide the best version of your story that we can. And so, we will edit that so that it is told in the most entertaining and sort of efficient way possible." That's the idea.'

I'm with Matt. I choose the people who write the best books, have done the most to save the planet with their food or have the most to say about their subject. I've already picked out the good guys. Once the interview has been secured, my interviewees know that they're in a safe space. It doesn't mean that I won't challenge them, and I may decide not to edit out the silence in which they consider how to answer. If it doesn't work as a question or it feels manipulative in some way, I'll simply cut it out. But it does mean that, once I've done my research and planned my show, I can record almost as-live, recording no more than forty minutes for a thirty- to thirty-five-minute episode of well-researched content with very little work to do in post-production.

Editing is always a creative process though. It's a sculpting of good material to make something great. It's about what you can take away and what you can add. For Hana Walker-Brown, after the connection is made between interviewer and interviewee: 'The storytelling, the music, the sound – it's all in the edit. It's deliberately designed to take you under and compel and keep you there, to pull you even further down.' But according to Helen Zaltzman of *The Allusionist* and *Answer Me This!!*, there's an argument to say that editing is a kind of dishonesty. And that there's nothing wrong with that: 'Every form of media or art has some editing in it,' she told me. 'You look at a painting; not every thought the painter has had is in that painting. Some of them have been removed or painted over. Every film, every journalistic article, there is some form of reduction in content.'

While I record as-live, editing very little out other than to tidy up and make points clearer, Helen and Olly Mann deliberately over-record for *Answer Me This!!*. Helen edits after Olly has listened up to three times on his headphones. 'It's usually ninety minutes, and that'll be cut to fifty,' she said. 'We might save a bit over for a future show.' Olly told me it was more like three hours and Helen settled on 'maybe two, sometimes. For *The Allusionist* I'll record for one to three hours and use fifteen to twenty minutes.' But it's the point of honing the final product that makes the difference between the so-so podcast and the professional piece that will have listeners sticking with you for over a decade. It's the skill of making something work instead of hoping for the best. 'Why do people think that podcasts should just be free rein of all the blah de blah coming out of your mouth?' she said.

Helen was a book editor before Olly Mann persuaded her to join him on his adventure in podcasting with *Answer Me This!!* in 2007. 'I was mostly proofreading and doing indexes, which is a very boring job,' she told me. 'But I liked the feeling of having a finite amount of material and just having to make it the best version of itself. I found that easier than actually creating the material. And then when it came to podcasting, I felt that same principle applied.'

She admits that she doesn't like editing at all. But the joy of podcasting for her and for all of us is that once you've mastered your mic technique and done your preparation, it's about what happens in the room. Cressida Ward of Food Tryb says that being in the moment will get you the best content. 'It's just about having more of a conversation,' she said. 'Don't be afraid to have an input and ask more questions and let that conversation spiral. I think it makes it more natural for the guest as well. I think that's really important at first. Having a conversation is actually much nicer to listen to and you enjoy it more.'

With storytelling skills and a good interview technique, the edit can be very straightforward. I've rarely compressed a track or used any post-production techniques other than Auphonic's automated noise and hum reduction and LUFS mastering.

In the next chapter, we'll find out how great storytelling and subtle editing created one of the most successful podcasts in Britain.

POD POINTS

- When does silence work?
- How creative do you need to be?
- Check your intention with your interview
- Recording as-live saves time in the edit

14

Podcast Gold

Occasionally a collision of opportunity, talent and timing creates something that no one had seen coming. *My Dad Wrote a Porno* is one of those podcasts that when it launched in 2015 had journalists giggling over their own headlines, early adopters texting their friends about their genius find and entrepreneurial podcast-investors stroking their hipster beards and considering a whole new way of counting the cash. It was the *kerching* moment in amateur podcasting. But it didn't start that way.

Spotting the moment

Jamie Morton, James Cooper and Alice Levine were perhaps better connected than most hobbyist podcasters. They had met at Leeds University and each had found work in the media, James in TV production, Jamie in acting (*Neighbours*, no less) and Alice was already a BBC Radio 1 DJ. Jamie told me how they had started 'making stuff' at university: 'We were mainly doing the student TV station,' he said. 'We learned on the go how to use a camera and how to edit and how to produce stuff and record. And then, from there, we've all ended up working in media together in various forms. But on the side, we've always tried to have little projects that weren't necessarily meant to be seen or anything like that, but stuff that kind of creatively kept our hand in, just to keep flexing that muscle, I guess.'

So, when Jamie revealed to his friends that his dad had shown him *Belinda Blinked,* the pornographic novel that he had been secretly writing under the name Rocky Flintstone, the trio's creative reflex leapt. A modern story of sex, erotica and passion, subtitled 'How the sexiest sales girl in business earns her huge bonus by being the best at removing her high heels', was never going to be the story; the inappropriate revelation, the passing of the text from father to son was the hook. 'That's the weirdest bit for me,' he laughed. 'Like, why would you send your son your porn? But I did read it, against my better judgement, and realised pretty quickly that it was unintentionally hysterical.' He took it to the pub to read to Alice, James and a group of their friends. 'And we just were killing ourselves laughing, weren't we guys?' he remembered as I took them back to the birth of the phenomenon. 'It's one of those things that immediately just landed and we were just all like, "This is gold".'

Alice found it particularly interesting and tested it out more widely. 'There aren't that many things that make you belly laugh and make you evangelise about it,' she said. 'We became a bit obsessed with this writing and told people about it. I think that that was our initial litmus test. We were like, is it something that makes other people laugh as much as it made us laugh? When we tell people about it, do they laugh? When we read them passages, do they lose it? And they did. And then I think that's when our skills in media possibly kicked in for how to make it a product.'

They were on to a winner. Aware of the success of *Serial* the previous year, they felt that podcasting was having its moment. Although their joint projects so far had mostly been on YouTube, audio worked with this one: 'We figured with the subject matter, it being pornography, we were like, no one's going to want to watch it particularly,' said Jamie. 'How would we even visualise it if they did? So, audio became the obvious thing to do.' And it was cheap. With just the three of them sitting around the kitchen table with microphones, a podcast was a no-brainer.

Taking your time

James explained how important it was that they didn't rush it. Keeping the Morton family happy guided the way to finding the right tone. 'Jamie's dad needed to be involved and happy that we were doing it,' he said. They spent three months 'really thinking about what it was going to be and making sure everything was in place,' Jamie told me. 'Because it was my dad and these are my best mates and they've known my family for ages, we were a little bit unsure. Would people find it as funny as we did? Did you have to know my dad to find it funny? Do you have to know us?'

This process of excavating hours' worth of material, working out tone and motivation in podcasting is a legacy of *This American Life*, and I asked the team how intentionally they had played with the notion of making a very clever form of narrative non-fiction sound like a homemade passion project. 'It was something that we were quite aware of from the beginning,' said Jamie. 'We wanted the listeners to feel like the fourth friend around the table with us, and not someone peering in through a window and eavesdropping on our conversation. We wanted to make it feel as inclusive as possible.' The team were clear about what they wanted to achieve. 'We didn't let the show find its feet within the first few episodes,' said Jamie. 'It really came out fully formed, and that was all of that initial prep that did that, I think.'

Formatting helped. With Jamie reading Rocky Flintstone's – aka his dad's – latest chapter in each episode and Alice and James squeamishly picking at the details with a cross between British reserve and childish hilarity, the listener knew where they were going. You didn't even need to listen to the other episodes, except of course its legion of fans did, with over 30 million downloads to date. When they introduced guests to the show, they even did that differently. 'Because it's never an interview,' Alice said. 'We don't get people on the show who are on the promo trail. It's just people who really love Rocky's work.' Emma Thompson, Daisy Ridley, Michael Sheen and

Elijah Wood are among the 'Belinkers', the podcast's own fan tribe, who couldn't wait to discuss the latest chapter with the team. 'We really tried hard to make it sound loose, if that makes sense,' said Alice. 'But we didn't want it to be an hour and a half of stream-of-consciousness. It's always followed the same format, and that's kind of a bit of chat, a bit of establishing our week, a bit of talking amongst ourselves, recapping where we were at and then diving into what is the heart of the podcast, which is the chapter.'

They know their limitations and work to their skills. Alice is realistic about who they are: 'We know that we're not professional comedians, but we think we can make this really funny, so let's give ourselves the best chance.' Their best chance was to use Jamie's skillset as a professional editor to distil an hour and a half of recording to thirty minutes of tight comedy. As a solo podcaster, I'm always thinking about the edit while I'm recording, ensuring that I have what I need, that I've got the answers to my questions and have filled all the gaps, because – crucially – any rambling will be cut. I asked if the team were conscious of this while recording. Jamie laughed, 'It's really funny. Sometimes those two will go off on a tangent and I'll kind of oddly glass over, and they'll be like, "He's already cut that out mentally. It's not even in the show." They know from my reaction to something if I've kind of checked out mentally.'

No rambling required

Jamie insists that rambling is not allowed. 'We're very aware of not waffling on about our own lives. I think one of the interesting things about the show and how it's evolved was that for Series One, we were actually quite strict with ourselves. We were like, look, it's called *My Dad Wrote a Porno*, it's about *Belinda Blinked*. Let's really give people that as the majority of the thing, and then as people get to know us over a few series, then we can start feeding more of ourselves into it because initially no one really knows who you are. If you throw all of your crap at somebody, they're not going to want to kind of go on that journey with you. So, we were quite careful about how much of ourselves we released to the audience.'

Alice was clear that they should be professional from the outset, to 'put your money where your mouth is, even if it's not literally money, but to put your time and energy where your mouth is and make it look like you mean business,' she said. They weren't apologetic: 'We wanted it to look like the real deal because we do care about this. We looked for an audience and we found an even bigger audience than we'd hoped for, but I think we definitely put the infrastructure in place for if it did take off. We'd commissioned music, we made sure we had a logo, we had a website, we had all of our social media in place. I think all of our experience to date on other productions had said to us, be consistent, you know, put it out on the same day, find your tone and stick to it. Know what you're making before you put it out.'

When to monetise

Although they were pretty sure that it was going to be a runner from the outset, they decided not to attempt to monetise the podcast in the first year. 'It was a real opportunity to audience-build, and get a community going,' said Jamie. I asked why advertising might have stood in the way. 'I think we felt it was off-putting,' he said, 'because there weren't loads of precedents. Obviously, podcasts had been around for a long time, but we were at the start of this renaissance, and I think we felt like perhaps we had to earn the right to have that interruption to the product.'

American readers, you're no doubt scratching your heads about the British reserve towards getting paid for genius. What can I say? It's a foible. Alice took over the spluttering: 'Even though it's a free product, we just weren't sure what the audience's expectation was. Every podcast I listen to now has adverts on it, and it doesn't even really register, but I think at the time we felt like it could be an impediment to people coming back. And that was just a guess. That wasn't really based on anything empirical, it was just our feeling that it might be a bit of an unpleasant listen.'

Jamie added that advertisers wouldn't touch them at first anyway. Advertising can be one of the more conservative of the creative industries and, well, who could blame them for holding them at arm's length? 'It was a tiny podcast that had just started . . . about pornography,' Jamie laughed. 'I don't think we were at the top of most buyers' lists to be honest!'

By the time they did get their first ad, podcasting had moved on. 'It had evolved to a point whereby having one of those host-reads almost legitimised your podcast; it kind of meant that you were a "proper" podcast,' said Jamie. 'You know, you were up there with *Serial* and *This American Life*! If you can get one of those, "This episode is brought to you by Hello Fresh or Squarespace – the classic Squarespace – or MailChimp", you know it really felt like you'd arrived as a podcast. In an odd way, it legitimises your show and makes it one of the bigger shows.'

Smoke and mirrors; it's all part of the game in the Wild West of Podcastland where no one really knows how big you are. For the niche podcasters, size doesn't matter as much as the feedback in your Facebook group, but for anyone hoping to make a buck out of their pod, adverts and/or sponsorship – however small – are an essential part of the look.

Support from your host

The Swedish tech giant Acast was quick to spot this Wizard of Oz syndrome and when they first launched in the UK they offered a free piggyback to a number of early British podcasts that they felt had the right credentials, whether it was a great idea or a celebrity host. The *delicious.* podcast, Leon's *How to Eat to Save the Planet* and *The Borough Market Podcast*, with potentially ready-made audiences, were all given the golden ticket. Acast pioneered the practice of dynamically inserting ads into podcasts. 'We don't mind if your show is absolutely huge or absolutely tiny,' CEO Ross Adams told techcrunch.com in 2018. 'The model we have allows a serious mainstream publisher like the BBC to monetise – or a bedroom podcast hobbyist.'

Making money

It wasn't until the second year of *My Dad Wrote a Porno* that the team finally started earning money. It wasn't their priority, and they were lucky enough to have excellent jobs of their own. It gave them the time and security to play with the project. But pretty soon the world just couldn't get enough of *My Dad Wrote a Porno* and perhaps because its success was carving new lanes on roads barely even travelled yet in Podcastland, the team were hanging out the window grabbing at whatever fruits they chose. James puts its abundance at *Serial's* door: 'Podcasting had been around for years, but it was having this second wave with the success of Serial. And I don't think its potential had quite been tapped into yet. There were certain opportunities coming our way and we were thinking, *Oh okay . . .*' The book of the podcast was first published by Gallery Books in 2017 but James said that they were already thinking that there could be other iterations, even a multimedia experience. A live show followed, with gigs in the most iconic venues in the world from the Albert Hall to Sydney Opera House, and European, Canadian and US tours packing houses full of millennials. *Kerching* indeed. 'I don't think we quite anticipated the scale of success the show has had,' said James rather humbly.

The team has learnt how to strategise and plan while keeping what James calls 'whatever feels right for the product' at the heart of it. Jamie agreed: 'We make sure that whatever the new iteration, it has a real purpose for being in that format, whether it's the HBO show or the live shows. We never want to do something just because we've been offered it. It really has to be right by Belinda,' he laughed. Alice explained that it is this sense of focus that drove the decision to produce just one series a year. 'It's special,' she said. 'And the source material's really special. And I think that we treat it that way whenever we spin it off into something else.'

These days they take the ads, but in true *Porno* style, they've reinvented the wheel. 'Jamie and I always joke about Alec Baldwin doing his Beef Mignon advert for Blue Apron,' James laughed. 'There's something slightly bizarre and amazing about that, about hearing him talk about peppercorn sauce. Podcast adverts have been pastiched so much. We try and place advertising in a way that doesn't cut through the content, but I feel like people are very forgiving and understanding. We're very careful about what we do.' Jamie agreed: 'I think there is an understanding that you do need to pay for content. People are kind of getting that a show like ours actually takes quite a lot of planning and producing. And I think people are quite respectful of that.'

The big podcasters have followed America's pioneers all the way to the bank, but by doing so, they have opened the door to an endless supply of opportunities for contra deals (p. 177) for the rest of us. As we'll find out in the next section, podcasters can think laterally about what they need from a sponsor, and what their podcast can deliver in return.

But the lesson from the *My Dad Wrote a Porno* team is something that money can't buy: the authenticity of their friendship and the ability to spot a story when it lands in your lap. We can learn an enormous amount from their process, their intention and their entrepreneurial chutzpah, but if your best mate's dad isn't writing an erotic novel (badly), you're going to have to look hard to find such podcast gold.

<<<*Listen to the full interview on* How to Grow a Pod.>>>

TECH talk

Jamie Morton wrote: 'The mics we use are Samson C01Upro, whatever that means lol.'

POD POINTS

- Take time to work out what you want from your podcast before launch
- Try out the ideas on your mates: what makes something funny?
- It takes skill to sound relaxed!

PART III:
Show Me the Money

15

Beer Money

Most podcasts these days are passion projects, nerdy, niche hobbies or just a bit of fun. But if small and cosy is about community and authenticity, telling yourself that size doesn't matter is about as effective as promising not to check your Instagram likes. The truth is that you can have it all if you want it, but many podcasters simply don't. They may not have the time – the day job is too taxing and their podcast is their moment in the shed at the end of the day – while, increasingly, some businesses use it as a twenty-first century intranet to communicate with colleagues. It's just not always about the money.

But if you do want to test out your value in this interesting new market, here is a good place to start. There are more ways to monetise your podcast than sponsorship or advertising, and in the next chapters, we find out how even the most humble of podcasters may be missing a trick. Small is beautiful in Podcastland. 'If you're getting 134 downloads per episode, you're doing better than 50 per cent of all podcasters,' says South African entrepreneur, business coach, events guru and podcaster Jason Allan Scott. 'That's how many hobbyists there are out there.' He tells me that the figure comes from the VP of Libsyn, and I believe him. But interestingly Tom Rossi, co-founder of Buzzsprout, one of the most popular hosts among amateur podcasters, told Podchaser in August 2020 how the breakdown of total number of downloads in the last thirty days looks for his community:

- 98 downloads puts you in the top 50 per cent of podcasts

- 302 downloads puts you in the top 25 per cent of podcasts
- 982 downloads puts you in the top 10 per cent of podcasts
- 2373 downloads puts you in the top 5 per cent of podcasts
- 14,959 downloads puts you in the top 1 per cent of podcasts

It's interesting to note that Buzzsprout's 2020 figures are significantly lower than *The Feed*'s assessment of the downloads data in 2019, which suggests that there could be more podcasts diluting the audience's attention, but that it's easier to get to the top.

Jason Allan Scott says being in the top 50 per cent is podcasting gold. He knows what he's talking about after his books and his ability to harness the power of profit in a podcast have made him a fortune. He was voted the most influential man in events three times by Haymarket Media. His story is quite remarkable and well worth a listen on *How to Grow a Pod*. Niche podcasts are his bread and butter, and he says that they could be yours too. He tells his clients that their passion projects are where the money is. 'Niches to riches,' he tells me with a wink as we record the podcast episode via Zoom, 'double-ending' with my H4N and his Audio Technica Atr2100 microphone.

Monetising podcasts is Jason's main goal, and he believes that even the most niche of podcasters are interested in profit. I told him at the beginning of our interview about the book. 'Smart,' he said. 'It's one of the ways we talk about monetising a podcast.' I splutter in a rather British way that I didn't imagine charging anyone to listen, and he laughed. 'You'll be using your podcast as proof of expertise, to find organic traffic which will be driven back to you which in turn will have your listener grab their phone, find you, buy your book, look to see where you're speaking, attend your events, rush over to other social media platforms to see what other brilliance you're spouting. And so you profit from a podcast.' I hadn't even seen what was right under my nose.

The ability to spot an opportunity is hard-wired into the average podcaster's DNA. We're naturally entrepreneurial, looking laterally at ways to book guests and create our content, but, like most people, we can find it hard to put a value on our own heads, particularly for a passion project. Yet profit is everywhere in podcasting, according to Jason, and the niche podcaster doesn't have to think small. 'Unlike in marketing where we talk about demographics, the more niche you can be in podcasting, the deeper you can go, the more reaction you get,' he told me. But for many niche podcasters, the word can hide a lack of confidence. 'Most people say that they're doing it for fun,' he says. 'But they say that because of their fear of failure.' While success in podcasting can be measured simply by meeting your heroes, it can also mean leveraging your expertise to launch a new career with fewer overheads and more control; yet most niche podcasters dismiss it as a hobby, a bit of fun.

Guilty. I worked on a podcast that paid me less than the minimum wage for *years* because it was such fun. But it did take me all over the world at the PR's expense and right into the kitchens of my heroes thanks to introductions made by the magazine. It made me an expert in my field, attracting speaking events at WOMAD, Latitude and the British Library Food Season. It leveraged interest in a book of mine that began life as a piece of academic research and would otherwise have languished in university libraries but was able to burst with voices from the food world right into the centre of my mainstream foodie community. I hold podcasting retreats at my home; I teach the NCTJ (National College for the Training of Journalism) course. I was even approached to write a book about how to make and grow a successful podcast!

It's imposter syndrome, the fear of flying that holds most people back from doing what they really want to do in life, and Jason has heard it all before. 'You're hoping for social proof to say, "I'm as cool in this field as the people who I bring on my show". We're so scared to say that to the world.' He suggests breaking it down. 'So, call it a project. Call it a season. Say, you know what? It's eleven episodes, Netflix-style, or twenty-two episodes, HBO style, and I'm just going to try something. The minute you say that, you take away the fear of failure.

It's just a project.' The average podcaster, he told me, completes between three and five episodes before giving up. That's more than 40 per cent of over a million podcasts, 400,000 shows with fewer than five episodes. He says that it's called 'podfade' and even if he's made it up, I buy it. 'It's because they had no idea what success looks like,' he told me. 'They had no idea what they were doing. They were too scared to say, "It's only a project and it's only going to live this long".' They had no idea, he says, that they can create value out of scarcity.

Yet Podcastland shares a culture with the Land of Oz where smoke and mirrors are everywhere and anything is possible – unlike YouTube. Jason works with content creators across platforms and told me that clients come to him with only three subscribers and seven views on YouTube, cringing with embarrassment. 'Everyone can see it!' they tell him. 'At least with podcasts, you can't see how many people are listening!' he laughed. He persuades his clients to follow the advice that he was given by Noah Kagan, Facebook's thirtieth employee, who in turn got it from Mark Zuckerberg himself. He tells them to choose just one metric of success per season and to chase it. 'You start with the three subscribers,' he told me, using the hapless YouTuber's example. 'Next time you'll get six and you've gone up 100 per cent! And then you get twelve and that's another 100 per cent. That's what you do in podcasting. You chase progress not perfection.'

It's the big numbers that set an impossible standard. 'They hear 150 million downloads for Lewis Howes, 200 million from Tim Ferriss or Joe Rogan just gets a $100 million deal, and they think that's what success looks like.' Beginners need to start with a different success metric. 'Maybe it's a family member who now knows who you are, that you really love birds and you are the auditory aviary person who everyone should listen to. And that's your metric for your first season. And your second season, maybe it's owning traffic, getting an email address. Your third season, maybe you get invited somewhere. Just one metric every time you attack something. And you just keep going until you hit that metric, and then you scale up, scale up, scale up.'

Building an audience

According to Jason, there are just twenty-one ways to build an audience. He told me about his favourite, the 'cheese grater effect'. 'You take a plate, add a grater to it and nothing happens. You take a piece of cheese and you add it to the plate and nothing happens. You take another piece of cheese and you add it to the plate and now there's too much cheese.' He continued the analogy as I tried to stay with it. 'So, we think of the plate as the multitude of syndication opportunities out there. It's iTunes, it's Libsyn, it's Stitcher, it's Google Play, it's iHeartRadio, etc. The piece of cheese is your influencer, your expert, the person who already has an audience, a following. You're the grater and your job is to bring that cheese to you and talk to them.'

I'm shifting in my seat as I picture myself as the grating personality in this analogy, slicing or crumbling the big cheeses of the food industry. Neither side is looking good, but I bear with his metaphor. As the cheese falls on the plate, so their expertise is distributed to the audience, but none of it would happen without the cheese grater. I get it; the audience is hungry for the morsels of wisdom that they're listening for, and if they like the way I grate the cheese, they'll come back for more. They know that they'll get fed. And as the Big Cheese heads off for the next grating, those who stay to nibble of the crumbs know that there's more quality stuff to come. The fans of your guests will stay with you if they like what you do. You're in their tribe. 'Every time you bring on one new listener, you'll probably get ten new listeners,' said Jason. 'And if you do a great job, you'll get ten new subscribers. And if you're *really* good at what you do, you'll have ten new fans. And that's all you need: a thousand true fans who will follow you anywhere in the world, who will buy your books, come to your events and who can't wait to tell their family and friends how great you are.'

When Jason set about studying the (very few) podcasts which

were making a million dollars or more, he found the same advice from each: monetise from day one. 'Give your listeners a reason to keep going, keep giving them value, whether that's a Patreon page, a PayPal, a T-shirt, a speaking engagement, a book. Give them a way to be fans.' He did just that. His book *The Eventrepreneur* did 'really well' and when he was invited to apply for the Top 100 Small Businesses in the UK awards, he thought that he had nothing to lose. 'I had no overheads other than my hosting bill,' and as he made his considerable income from podcasting alone, it was a no-brainer.

Turning your audience into your fans

How he found his audience and gave them an opportunity to support him is a wonderful story. His enthusiasm is infectious. '*You* love what you're doing and *they* love what you're doing. They *want* to support you,' he said of your would-be fans. 'You need a thousand people who love you to spend £1000 over a year and you've got six figures.'

Earbuds give podcasting presenters a unique opportunity to be in your body, and that's a power not to be messed with. If authenticity is the key to success in podcasting, as endless surveys have found, Jason Allan Scott is the master. Even admitting to his fans that he hadn't a clue about men's underwear added to his fans' commitment. They love his entrepreneurial mojo. 'You are the voice inside their heads,' he said. 'There's a responsibility to that. And you can pass on joy and sadness and human stories.'

Like many of the most successful storytellers, Jason often uses the 'hero's journey' or the 'epiphany bridge' in his interviews. There are certain steps, he tells me, to turning every guest into a storyteller. 'Some of us do it so naturally, that we don't even notice the extrinsic, the intrinsic, the *aha* moment, the time when the world was against me, the rising again, the phoenix from the ashes.' It's when we see this narrative arc in radio, in films and on TV, explained Jason, that we realise that this is the story of being human.

In the next chapters, we'll meet the podcasting pioneers who have found new ways to make money out of their passion projects by making it up as they've gone along.

TECH talk

Jason says he uses a Heil PR40 'if I want to sound like I'm right inside your head. If I want it to sound like we're having a conversation, I use this Audio Technica Atr2100. It's an incredible bit of kit and under £70.

'It's plugged into a Rode Rodecaster Pro which is a wonderful bit of kit. [It has] everything you need . . . to be a professional podcaster. You can link up to four different mics, four different headphones. You can change the volume. You can add sound effects. It's a full-on mixing desk but I can link it to my Apple, my phone, I can Bluetooth it to my other devices. It's very light so I can throw it in my backpack, throw in a couple of mics, throw in a pair of headphones and then I run around and I can plug this in pretty much anywhere.

'But if I am on the move, I usually take a TestCam DR40 with two microphones and one headset and a SiM card for all my roving interviews.

'Remotely, I use Skype with ECam which records everything the moment anyone calls in.

'Brett, my producer in North Carolina, uses Audition.'

POD POINTS

- Choose just one metric of success per season and chase it
- Tap into the communities of your heroes
- You only need a thousand true fans
- Give fans an opportunity to support you

16

The Expert

There are many ways to make your money out of podcasting, and as podcasters themselves keep inventing ever new ways, there will be many more to come. Entrepreneurial, media-savvy hobbyists who have found their true calling in podcasting will do all they can to make their passion project pay. Becoming an expert in your field could be an answer.

Olly Mann and Helen Zaltzman were among the first successful podcasters in Britain when they started *Answer Me This!!* in 2007. Olly told me how, as a twenty-five-year-old, while he was putting on a play at the Edinburgh Festival in 2006, a mind bomb went off which would set him on the path to becoming one of Britain's first podcasting experts. 'It was a play about blogs and attracted press made up of bloggers and podcasters,' he said. 'I'd heard about podcasting but I'd never downloaded one.' He spotted something new happening in the garden of the Underbelly where a tribe of 'nerds with pony tail, mini disc and clip-on mic' were interviewing him and other performers, and without a commission for a paper or any major bit of kit, seemed to be making it up as they went along. This was a different way of communicating to a tribe of interested fans, and apparently easy to pull off. Olly wanted in. 'They were pioneers,' he told me, 'but they were literally making podcasts about how to use Windows!' He realised that he could use the same process to make entertainment programmes without having to ask anyone's permission. He could do it all himself. 'I thought that there was a niche here for independent podcasters to match the efforts of the kind of thing the *Guardian* were doing,' he told me.

In 2005, Guardian Unlimited, the newspaper's innovative multi-platform arm, had commissioned Ricky Gervais with Stephen Merchant and Karl Pilkington to present *The Ricky Gervais Show* in a million-pound deal. It had started life as a weekly show in August 2001 on the radio station *Xfm* until GU's twelve-episode deal, and would go on to break records for its number of downloads. It appeared in the *Guinness World Records 2007* for the world's most downloaded podcast with an average of 261,670 downloads per episode during its first month and was signed up as a TV show for American giant HBO in 2010. It was a game-changer. Emily Bell, editor in chief of Guardian Unlimited said, 'GU has been experimenting with podcasting over the past year but this represents the start of a much bigger commitment to using different digital formats which give our users the best content in the most convenient way.' It was so new that in the note to editors on the press release in September 2005, GU had to explain what a podcast was.

It would open the door for traditional newspapers to experiment with embedded video and audio in this new online playground, although it would be BBC Sounds that would most successfully occupy the podcasting platform fifteen years on. This was before YouTube had even got out of bed, and fortune was favouring the brave with endless new spaces to play with. 'I was doing what a twenty-five-year-old would now do if they were on TikTok,' Olly told me.

Olly was born to be on radio. His appearance on Radio 4's *My Teenage Diary* revealed that he had groomed himself for a life of thinking aloud, but he would have to get past the curators to be allowed in. He said that podcasting was more than an opportunity to do it himself; it was about being able to 'experiment and be shit'. Hospital radio felt 'a bit low-grade' and community radio barely existed then. 'I couldn't see how else you can get on radio,' he told me. 'So this was a way of practising being on radio without being on radio.'

Along with university chum and fellow radiohead Helen Zaltzman, Olly would launch his masterplan with *Answer Me This!* in 2007, a 'geeky, intellectual, punky' podcast in which he and Helen answer listeners' questions on anything from factual to philosophical to personal issues. By 2009, it was listed in the *Guardian*'s top 10 comedy podcasts in the world and by 2011 it had won a gold award at the Sony Radio Academy Awards. He says that Helen was the obvious foil for his comedy after he had appeared as a regular guest on her student radio show when they were both at Oxford. 'I always felt good when I was talking to her,' he told me. 'The comedy just came naturally.' She was also rather handy with the technical side of things; when Olly and I talked in the summer of 2020, he still had never edited a single show. He also knew that Helen could do with another string to her bow at that time. While he had gone straight into working in TV entertainment after university, she was doing 'weird jobs like proofreading and writing other people's books'. It was a match made in podcast heaven. 'Everything happened quite organically,' he said. 'The job delineation was always quite clear, actually. Helen did the editing – pushing the buttons – and in return for what was an extra day's work a week my job was to do the publicity and to try to get an audience for the show.'

They were clear who the audience should be: 'A kind of version of us as sixth-formers,' he said. 'We were thinking, *What would an 18-year-old who has a curiosity about the world and a slightly sardonic sense of humour – what would they like?*' Happily, his day job involved thinking along the same lines. As a researcher for BBC 2's *Culture Show*, he was charged with following new trends, the latest bands and up-and-coming artists. 'This was the era when in terms of social media, Myspace was just becoming a thing,' he said. 'Kate Nash had just broken out and Lily Allen was around. So I'd piggy-back on lots of Myspace profiles, people like The Kooks. I'd reach out to all of their friends and tell them about *our* Myspace page.'

There's a theme among the podcasting pioneers I interviewed for this book and one I recognise from my own multi-media background. The TV and radio producer – particularly the freelancer – has an entrepreneurial creativity that adds another dimension to their podcasting expertise. They know how a story works and how to bring listeners to it through social media teasers. And they make it fun, which attracts the followers even more. Olly says that he individually targeted the two hundred people from The BRIT School who liked The Kooks. 'I either sent them a message or invited them to join our page or something,' he said. 'I cultivated a group that way.' He knew that it wasn't the most efficient use of his time and that it accounted for about 5 per cent of their audience, but he showed his media savvy in fishing where the fish are – even if it was a fairly small pond. He followed it up with a weekly mailshot, cheekily blind carbon copying in anyone he had met in radio and TV.

For those without a little black book of their own, the updated version is that great Rolodex in the cloud known as Twitter and Instagram. Never have so many famous influential people been so easy to write to. Use a hashtag to find the conversations that influencers in your subject area are part of and jump on in.

Creating the media event

A well-timed publicity stunt piqued the interest of the press and established a place for *Answer Me This!* in the podcasting hall of fame. Again, Olly's media sensibility led him to create a checklist.

1. Timing: 'We decided that we would target the first week of January when everyone had just come off Christmas and there was nothing to write about. Lazy journalists just want something easy.'

2. Spoon feed the media: 'We thought, *We'll do a video and a press*

release. We'll put ourselves forward for an interview, and put some facts in there that people didn't know and we'll present ourselves as experts.'

3. Create a stunt: They decided to become experts in how to crack the podcast charts. Which meant doing it themselves with *Answer Me This!*. 'We realised it was very hard to break into the iTunes chart in the UK simply because of the big entrants that were around at the time: the *Guardian, The Times*, the BBC. But theoretically the whole system was set up in a way where anyone – an independent producer or a big broadcaster – should be able to crash into the iTunes charts. We realised the smaller the country, the more opportunity there was to cheat the algorithms.'

At the time, iTunes had just ten international locations with a podcast chart. Luxembourg, one of the smallest sovereign states in Europe, was one of the ten. 'Apple's HQ was based in Luxembourg for Europe,' said Olly. 'But it's literally a postbox on a street in Luxembourg. And so we thought it would be funny to go to that postbox and petition iTunes to get into the chart. We spent the day in Luxembourg drumming up publicity to try and get people to download our show.' Filming it all on a mini DV ('It looks like it was filmed on a toaster. This was way before smartphones'), they handed out biscuits and even got themselves a guest spot on the English-language breakfast radio show. 'It's surprisingly easy to make yourself a celebrity in Luxembourg,' he laughed. It worked! They reached number 3 in the Luxembourg charts overnight. 'That was a great end to the video,' Olly told me. They spent Christmas editing the video, writing the release with the headline 'We've cracked Luxembourg', and had it on the news desks for the first week of 2008. Sky News, 5 Live and the *Daily Telegraph* all lapped it up. They made *Answer Me This!* a phenomenon in podcasting and turned Olly and Helen into media internet experts.

Olly acknowledges their privilege in being able to pull it off, not just in Luxembourg but as they grew their reputation as the king and queen of podcasting; they had disposable income, contacts and the kind of confidence that comes from an Oxford University education. But he says it was more than that. 'We were kind of punky,' he said. 'Not just because we were making it at home and there were swear words in it and we talked about sex. We were punky because we really didn't look like the other twenty-five-year-olds, the slick, very boring, looks-driven twenty-somethings in the media at the time. Helen and I would go for meetings with production companies where some junior researcher had found our podcast and thought we might be good on the telly, and there'd always be a whiteboard with "George Lamb, Alex Zane", people like that. And then at the bottom it would say "Helen and Olly?" And it's like, who are these fat, posh, Jewish kids?'

Since then, Olly has achieved his dream of having his own radio shows on LBC Radio 4 and appearing as a gadget expert on Radio 2. In *Web 2009* and *Web 2010,* he and Helen predicted the next year's tech trends on BBC 5 Live, the first time British podcasters had been given their own radio show on the BBC. They are still professional podcasters: Helen presents *The Allusionist* and the Veronica Mars recap podcast, *Veronica Mars Investigations* as well as *Answer Me This!* with Olly, while he presents *The Modern Mann* and *The Week Unwrapped* (see p.37 for his producer Matt Hill's story of this podcast). He says that none of it would have happened without *Answer Me This!*. 'I always had a latent ambition to be on mic but I was quite nervous and shy in a way that most people are in their late teens/early twenties, and I pretended that I would be satisfied working behind the scenes on stuff for about ten years.' By 2011, he was a successful freelance broadcaster. 'It wasn't because the opportunity wasn't there. It was just a certain resistance to putting myself out there. Podcasting gave me the confidence to contact people in radio and say "Yeah, people are interested in what I have to say and how we're saying it".'

For all the *Star Trek* nerds and the nineties music geeks in Podcastland, there's a radio station, local newspaper or even national broadcaster just waiting to make you their go-to person as an expert in your subject. Learning from Olly's chutzpah could give you that big break.

As early adopters, he and Helen were stumbling over the foundations of a brand new podcasting business. Their first podcast host, which initially charged them around $7 per month, issued a bill for over $1,000 when, after around sixty episodes, their download figures began to fly. They hadn't read the small print. 'It was because we were using up their bandwidth, and because back then memory cost more than it does now, so some computer in Austin, Texas was working overtime for us,' said Olly. Libsyn was the only host they could find at the time that allowed unlimited downloads. The playing field has since been levelled, and they are still with Libsyn.

But they still had to settle the bill, and it scared them. The original host agreed on a compromise of $200, but Olly and Helen knew that they couldn't afford to make another mistake. Without a safety net, they couldn't afford to do the show. They decided to put thirty episodes behind a paywall. A PayPal transaction would send a link to the website where their fans could download the episodes. But it revealed a new idea. 'We quickly realised there were loads of benefits to doing it,' said Olly. 'One was taking our early terrible work off the internet! People hearing us for the first time were not hearing episode one, which was obviously appalling; they were downloading episode forty which was much better. Secondly, once they had become a fan of the show by listening to episodes forty through sixty, they could then go back and want to listen to episode one like it was some rare collectible Bob Dylan album. So, there was value to be extracted in them paying for it. They wanted to get something rare, and were appreciating the content even though it wasn't very good. And thirdly we realised there was a revenue stream there, particularly for

American listeners. We realised quickly that Americans *want* to give you money. I mean they were writing to us saying, "How can we contribute to the show?" That just wasn't part of our culture at all.'

It was this that underpinned his plan to monetise *The Modern Mann*. But much as he liked the American attitude towards money, he wasn't a fan of their slick sponsor reads. He knew his producer Matt Hill needed payment and he could see that there was a way of making money from podcasting, but he wanted to do it his own way. He had an idea. 'I came up with "beer money". When I was in the right place – the Edinburgh Festival or the iTunes Festival or Glastonbury – the kind of place where people listen to *Answer Me This!*, if someone recognised me, they would come up to me and say, "Thank you so much for giving me the last ten years of content. I owe you a beer."' It was an idea he could take online. 'We set up a form that was the price of a beer, but actually it defaulted to a regular monthly payment unless you chose to make it a one-off payment. About 50 per cent of people were happy to make that a recurring subscription effectively.' He opted not to use Patreon, the creator-pay platform that was founded by Stanford University roommates Jack Conte, a musician, and Sam Yam, a computer scientist, in 2013. 'I've always done my own thing and I don't want to be one of those guys being like, "Hey, check out our Patreon." I just don't want to do that.' And with the form that he built himself, he bumped into another revelation. 'I'm doing customer service,' he told me. 'So, if people want to cancel their beer money subscription or amend it, they have to email me. And you can feel their surprise that it's me – which is bizarre because what do they think? That we have some South Korean call centre somewhere? And when I say, "Thanks so much for supporting my show. How much would you like to amend your payment to? And do you mind me asking what your favourite episode was?", and sign it *Olly*, people were saying, "Oh my God, it's you! I never thought it would be you!" It's that personal touch for me is what podcasting is all about.'

Olly, the tech expert, believes that the next technological moment in podcasting will be brought about by Libra, Facebook's proposed blockchain-based digital currency that was delayed in early 2020 after resistance from regulators. According to Bloomberg and tech site The Information, it is now considering a system with digital versions of established currencies, including the dollar and the Euro. Olly explained why it could be a game-changer for podcasters: 'If the average listener is about forty and so are the people who are making the shows, then they are all on Facebook,' he said. He reckons that if Facebook launches a listening platform to rival Spotify, audio will become as essential as video. 'They then introduce a financial mechanism which is as easy as pressing "Like", and you can send me a pound for listening to my show. That to me does seem transformative.'

Currently, 1 per cent of Olly's podcast audiences are donating but with an audience of over 100,000, it is still valuable. 'But if on Facebook, you could get 30 per cent of that audience giving you a pound, then obviously that's substantially more valuable,' he said. 'I do wonder if there is something in digital currency and the conversion of that with social media and audio, that could make that whole system so much more straightforward.' He believes that people would not be deterred by Facebook, a corporate giant, acting as the intermediary in such a transaction. 'I think people would feel the intimate connection because it's me as an individual.' It's more a direct relationship between what you like and who made it. 'It pivots the industry a little away from sponsorship,' he explained. 'Why do I have to talk about mattresses when I can just get paid to talk to you about the thing you're interested in?'

With a book deal in 2010, Olly and Helen's brand had real value and they could begin to command good sponsorship income and leverage their position to get to where they wanted to be. Olly retraced the steps. 'All the economic models have changed and evolved as the whole thing has progressed. In 2010/2011 my goal was, "I'll become a rent-a-gob. I can make money out of public appearances and use that leverage to get other people to download my stuff." But that isn't what it is any more. It's evolved further. I've realised the power of podcasting and the incredible shallowness of telly. Now I want to use TV and radio to do [those] things that I find interesting as projects when they come up, when people approach me, but all of my energy goes into podcasting because I think it's the best mechanism actually that's been invented for what I want to do. It's so satisfying as an entrepreneur and a self-employed start-up to be able to live, to be able to pay my mortgage and feed my children from podcasting. Doing that is incredible.'

As we move into the world of social media and influencers in the next chapter, Olly and Helen feel as if they're part of a bygone era, the podcasters who pop over to 5 Live and Radio 4 instead of appearing on Instagram lives. But it's the sheer chutzpah of Olly Mann and Helen Zaltzman that makes their story so compelling and it's packed with lessons for us all. As the earliest of Britain's podcasting pioneers, they could be said to have created the quirky culture which sets us apart from our American colleagues with its beer money and DIY emails, but like the *My Dad* team, there's method underpinning their madness. Storytelling runs through their veins but it's the rigorous attention to detail that has made them full-time professional podcasters.

<<<*Listen to Olly Mann on* How to Grow a Pod.>>>

POD POINTS

- Leverage your experience to become an expert in your field
- Attract media attention: consider your own stunt
- Put a value on your expertise

17

The Influencers

This morning, my breakfast was interrupted by a knock on the door. A box labelled 'This Way Up' is always a good sign. It usually means wine. As the socially distanced delivery man photographed my box of goodies from gourmet Greek grocer Odysea, so did I. A post on Instagram is my way of saying thank you.

I hadn't expected the box of organic olive oils, manouri cheese and Karavitakis Klima wines from Crete from Odysea, but I was about to do a remote lunch with MasterChef 2019 winner Irini Tzortzoglou for *Cooking the Books* and we had been chatting about where I would get the Cretan wines essential for our feast. 'Leave it to me,' she said with a wink. I called her to thank her for organising the package from the brand she works with regularly. She laughed. 'Until you eat the food and drink the wine, you cannot talk about it.' She's right; authenticity is the key to good content.

It's not the first time that Odysea have sent me a bumper pack of delicious Greek treats. I've had a coffee with the CEO and lunch with the PRs, and they have logged my deep interest in organic Greek food. My very first book was *The Mediterranean Health Diet* and I've been working on an idea of updating it for years. I've often interviewed the food writers Odysea support. I love the food memories of food writers from all over the world, but Greece has always held a special place in my heart. It is in Odysea's interest to keep a tab on all the content creators who love to post about their products. But it has to come from a place of trust.

Social media is an essential toolkit for podcasters, and Instagram can offer a particularly great way of telling the back story to your show. Back in 2010, Instagram was just another platform eager for space, but by 2012 it had been bought by Facebook and was well on its way to dominance. Early adopters were rewarded with an exponential rise in followers; if you were on Instagram by 2014 with something vaguely interesting to look at, you could rack up followers pretty easily. These days, the market place is rather more crowded, yet content creators – as 'influencers', the internet celebrities who have made their mark on Instagram as well as YouTube, prefer to be called – can earn a good living from promoting their lifestyle on social media.

The value of the micro-influencer

Becoming an influencer can bring you rewards you may never have dreamed of. With my few thousand followers, I'm known as a micro-influencer because of my small but engaged group of foodies. I have organically carved out a niche following in an often-chaotic space where conflicting content can make true communities hard to find. The clarity of a narrative is what brands are looking for. Mine is simple: I write and podcast about food, but my niche interests are in food writing and sustainability. My audience is hyper-engaged with the small community of A-list food writers who appear on my podcasts, and is interested in how I explore the links between food and climate change, food writing, identity and influence. My interest is their interest, in how to find new foods across the world while refusing to fly. I represent the foodie who cares about the planet, who wants to eat better to save the world, who cares about the back story. My struggle is their struggle. My finds are theirs too. I wrestle with the moral choice between taking a #staycation during a pandemic or supporting the food and tourism industry. They often want me to take the first step and report back. And brands that align themselves with the same issues are often happy to support me in cash or in kind.

Support can be dressed in many outfits on social media. A contra deal might involve swapping a sponsor read on your podcast for a call to action to join your mailing list. A story on your sponsor's Instagram with a 'swipe-up-to-listen' could offer a better return than a cash deal, if you're interested in the long game. As you grow your audience, you can grow your income with real opportunities for your brand partners.

Danny Lowney is managing director of influencer agency Sixteenth, and is watching with interest the potential of podcasting to become the next platform to monetise. He sees it as an inevitable part of the content creator's toolkit and encourages his influencers to diversify their content channels with a podcast. 'It's a relatively low-friction platform,' he said, referring to its ease of access, the immediacy of enjoyment with little effort. 'And it's been having a moment for a few years now. It just makes sense as a place to go.' Many of Danny's clients are fitness people who attract deals from sports brands. I suggested to him that a half-hour podcast series on health and fitness might be the perfect platform for this kind of sponsor. He agreed that it's a logical step but told me that it's not right for everyone. 'We find that most influencers are almost born for a specific platform. You might get very big on YouTube, and you may also grow a big following on Instagram, but you're really a YouTuber at heart. Or you might grow a big following on Instagram and also have a YouTube channel but really, you're born on Instagram. And the same goes for podcasts; some talent has become big from podcasts and they might be leaking out onto YouTube and Instagram, but we don't see a ton of them right now. Obviously, you have personalities like Joe Rogan who have become big from podcasting, and all their other stuff is separate, but those cases are few and far between.'

There are two different conversations that Danny has when he pitches a podcast to a brand. One is about performance marketing: 'We're all familiar with the dozen or so brands that you hear on pretty much every podcast,' he said, 'and they're there for performance marketing. They're there for impressions.' He is referring to the moment a listener finds their way to the site. 'It's just a media buy but it can be very lucrative if you have a lot of impressions and downloads and plays. It can be brilliant.'

The other is the 'branded-content conversation', a more creative opportunity for a brand (he cites eBay as an example) to work with talent or a production company on a series of content that helps to tell the brand's story. 'It's non-invasive,' he explained. 'Or at least that's the intention. The branded content can be more lucrative if you're very, very talented creatively and you've got a very strong concept, and if you're able to communicate brand messaging through some kind of narrative.'

He agrees with Jason Allan Scott about the power of the podcast to deliver an appropriate brand directly into the ears of the person who's most likely to buy its product. But it's more than matching brand with niche; Danny believes that the value of the hyper-engaged listener comes with the nature of the relationship between the listener and the person producing the content. 'Say I'm an influencer, I produce content and I have 1000 or 100 listeners,' he told me. 'The relationship I have with those 100 listeners is super important because if I have influence over those people, that's what I'm able to monetise with a brand. A brand shouldn't just be paying for a vanity metric, they should be paying for action and results.'

My favourite social media mantra, 'keep on keeping on', works with brands. Danny explained that it takes time for an influencer to build a relationship with their community, but if it works, it is particularly valuable. 'That's when we really remember that purchasing and marketing is really just word of mouth at scale,' he said. He gave me an example of how it works: 'If I was drinking a certain type of coffee and, just as we started recording, I said, "Oh, by the way, this coffee is so good you have to try it next time you're in Brighton", there's a very high chance that you'd try it out. And that's because we have a level of relationship. If I'm able to emulate a piece of that with hundreds of people, that is super valuable.'

The key to the success of the podcaster is authenticity that comes from the passion, the geekiness, the nerdiness, the idea of the single person soldiering on alone on their passion project. It's because we really care about our subjects that there's an authenticity about a podcaster that can't be bought. I asked Danny how he protects that quality in the content creators that he manages when there's money on the table. 'I'm not sure it's my job to keep someone authentic,' he told me, 'because I'm not sure that's actually possible. I think people are who they are. My job is to choose the right people so that that doesn't become an issue. That's the thing we're trying to get to the root of. Is this person motivated by an absolute buzz from creating an audience or a community, from getting a message saying, "I listened to that episode you did a few weeks ago and I went and tried that technique and it worked so well". If that's what the motivation is, that's really encouraging. I think it's just about the selection process.'

Danny's job is to build a client list interested in telling their stories with the help of his talent, and as the pool of podcasting talent grows, he agrees that it's only a matter of time before his clients look from YouTube and Instagram towards the podspace. Curating and nurturing that talent could be the key to the future of this exciting new relationship.

POD POINTS

- Court your Instagram following by posting about your podcast
- Micro-influencers have value
- Are you an Instagrammer or a YouTuber?

18

Crowdfunding

In this make-it-up-as-you-go-along world of podcasting, fortune favours the brave. And for the entrepreneurial go-getters with a surfeit of energy and creativity who so often find an outlet in podcasting, it's often where the rewards are.

Crowdfunding, the multi-platform campaign to raise varying amounts of money from friends, family and anyone who likes your idea, is the creative cousin to the plucky podcast. It's a fun way of making some noise about your passion project and bringing your listeners along with you on the ride to making it real. It's an investment that's more than cash; as you tease them with your trailer, feed them with your fundraising news and thrill them with your success, they're with you all the way. For those wanting to top up a grant or an existing fund, it can make the difference between a great idea and a New and Noteworthy podcast.

Chris Hogg is a playwright, poet, TED Talker and academic in social media at London's Goldsmith's and Royal Holloway University, where I co-taught with him recently. His podcast *Rathband* is an immersive audio experience that tells the story of the policeman blinded by rogue gunman Raoul Moat in July 2010 and won the BBC Audio Drama award in 2018. It was the first of his applications for Arts Council funding, and he received £8953.

His latest podcast, *Cassie and Corey*, is a drum 'n' bass musical about eating disorders, and was, again, part-funded by the Arts Council. 'I applied for £15,000,' he told me, 'and I was rejected the first time.' Arts Council applications are notoriously tough and the process requires you to drill down until you are crystal clear about what your artistic aims are and your plans for it long term.

But he did finally manage to get £7000 through Kickstarter and his own funds; as Chris explained, it was important to show the Council that he was raising at least a third of the £21,000 budget himself and another third of the money 'in kind'. Royal Holloway University had only just completed a multi-million-pound immersive sound studio and he was able to record there, which he says made the world of difference. 'But it did allow me to pay the actors,' he told me. 'And for me, that is the most important thing, that I'm creating work for people that have precarious lives. And that's what the Arts Council money is for, to try and get as many people work within the arts at a local level as possible. I think I achieved that. I'm really proud of *Cassie and Corey*. I think it's quite a special piece of work.'

Perhaps what also made *Cassie and Corey* stand out among the pile of applications and what attracted the crowdfunders through Kickstarter was Chris's personal relationship with the subject of the show. 'Food has always been an issue for me,' he told me. 'It is a panacea. It is something that smooths over the cracks, that stops me feeling angry.' His interest in eating disorders had already won him a small pot of funding to create a show in 2017 for Theatre 503. The research for the play sent him to St George's Hospital in Tooting to discuss the project with the hospital's head of ethics. He asked what kept her up at night. 'It's the pressure that's put on the NHS to treat people as if they are responsible for their own condition,' she said. 'So if they smoke or if they drink, or if they overeat, these are things that people are encouraged to look after themselves.' As she explained the complexity of some of the issues around eating disorders, Chris felt that his story was beginning to take shape.

St George's is the centre for bariatric surgery for teenagers, the process for fitting gastric bands. Its eating disorder clinic treats people with anorexia and bulimia and the clinically obese, which for Chris presented an interesting juxtaposition on which to centre his story. 'It seemed very interesting to me that if we could take the idea of people not caring for themselves around food, and the idea of taking people on a journey using the things that I could learn from the NHS, it would be a very interesting podcast.'

And so *Cassie and Corey* was born, in Chris's head anyway. Corey is a clinically obese teenager with a very unhealthy BMI of 60 and serious intracranial hypertension. On the eve of his bariatric surgery, he visits his friend Cassie, an anorexic teenager he met in the eating disorder clinic, on a stolen shopping scooter, and they head off on a night-time adventure to audition for The BRIT School. 'I'm really interested in writing for teenagers,' Chris told me. 'I think that they are so interesting as a group. They are full of energy and thought and passion and they need stories. They get a certain type of story from the TV, they get a certain type of story from YouTube, but I wanted them to get a certain type of story from listening to an immersive art form. Podcasting is the most immersive art form.'

Chris even walked from St George's to The BRIT School, which is where the story ends, taking notice of every single shop, every single sign. 'I tried to turn that into a kind of concrete poetry that's going through the heads of the characters as they're trying to get to their goal, which is to change their lives,' he told me. 'So, you're ticking a lot of boxes: you're teaching public awareness of an under-resourced area, perhaps in the public consciousness. You're looking at drum 'n' bass. You're putting lots of strange, ill-fitting ideas, mashing things up and creating something explosively new.'

For the Arts Council, it was spot on. 'The Arts Council is interested in trying to create art not only for hard-to-reach audiences,' said Chris, 'but also to create work for people that are perhaps under-represented within the arts community.' *Cassie and Corey* was using some of Britain's finest black young actors but also showcasing a drum 'n' bass band, Girls

Take Action or GTA, who provided the soundtrack and drove the narrative for a killer Kickstarter promotional video.

It took just three weeks for Chris to get to his goal of £5000 with Kickstarter. 'I think crowdfunding campaigns are really important,' he told me. 'They take effort, they take thought, but what they also do is they allow you to have that first chemical reaction between your idea and your potential audience. Whether you're a maker or a writer, it takes five or ten years to build up your core audience. But once you've done that, you have a group of people that support you in your new ideas and where you want to go.'

If Jason Allan Scott says that we only need 1000 fans who will follow and support us in everything we do, Chris says that it's their active investment that makes the difference. 'One of the first things that was ever crowdfunded was the base to the Statue of Liberty.' He told me the story about the gift from the French in 1885. 'So the Statue of Liberty arrived from Paris and it gets left on the quayside in New York. There are some financial disputes going on in the city about who is going to pay for this huge statue, and you have the other cities around saying, well, I'll have it. Chicago's going, "Yeah, please give it to us." And Baltimore's going, "We really, really want this. We're going to run a campaign."' Publisher Joseph Pulitzer decided to place an advertisement in his newspaper the *New York World* inviting readers to crowdfund for a base for the statue in exchange for each donor's name in the paper. One hundred and twenty thousand people donated more than $100,000 for a pedestal for the great Bartoli statue. 'And you can see pictures of the advert online,' said Chris. 'Everybody got involved, from shoeshine kids that had a dollar to big businessmen. Within a very short amount of time, they had raised the money for the pedestal.'

The crowdfunding process involves people in your work. 'You learn about your audience,' he said. 'You find out things about your subject matter that you never really knew about. People come out of the woodwork and say, "Hey, I can help you with this," or, "I can help you with that." People like exclusivity. They like to think of themselves [as being part of] projects they think are doing some good, that they are on a storytelling journey where they can also connect with each other.'

It sounds like a parallel universe where helpful people are falling over themselves to fund your work, but for Chris and many other entrepreneurial podcasts, it really works. Not only did he get the cash he needed, but he got the audience too. Within two months, his podcast had 5172 downloads.

A month after launch, *Cassie and Corey* was on iTunes' New and Noteworthy, which catapults podcasts into the public eye. But although it has a great back story and deserves to be there, it was Chris again who intervened to get it there. 'Trying to get it visible on iTunes or Spotify is one of the key aims,' he told me. 'You get listeners straight away so it's worth really trying to make that happen.'

He checked into LinkedIn to find the people in charge of editorial at iTunes and Spotify. 'I actually wrote to New and Noteworthy on iTunes,' he said. 'I knew that if you are prepared and make their job easy, you're much more likely to get some kind of reaction. So we had all the artwork ready exactly to specification [4320 x 1080 pixels, 72 dpi and colour space of RGB delivered in a PSD file] and we sent that with our request. We told them that we were working with some incredible black talent and that they needed to be showcased because of traditional reasons for under-representation. We said that it was for a niche audience and had been funded by the Arts Council. And it was something truly original. It was a drum 'n' bass musical about eating disorders. And that's a mashup, but that's a genre mashup. It's original. It hasn't been done before and the aim is to do some good.'

In the race to produce your podcast and grow an audience, its real worth can sometimes get lost, but Chris shows us how much fun you can have along the way. In the next chapter we learn to find the value in podcasting.

TECH talk

Chris uses a Yeti microphone. 'It sits very solid on my desk. It's got felt underneath and it's like a tank. It plugs in USB-style to my laptop. And what I like about it is that no matter what kind of vibrations are going into the room or to the house or from what angle, it seems to absorb them and give you a really solid sound.

'I've also been using a piece of software called Descript which allows you to transcribe multiple people in a conversation in the most seamless way I've come across thus far. So you might take your Zoom recording, or if you're using a clean feed recording, and you upload it and it automatically recognises each of the different speakers and allows you to give them a name.

And then within about five minutes, [Descript] transcribes the entire conversation. But the most amazing thing about it is that you can, once you've got the transcript, edit the word file transcript and it changes the audio file. So you're not having to stare at those wave forms and listen again and again. You're looking at some words on a page, which for someone like me who likes words, is brilliant. It just saves so much time and energy.'

POD POINTS

- Crowdfunding can build an audience before you've even launched
- Be clear about what your aims are
- Plan for maximum impact in your first eight weeks
- You only need a thousand fans!

19

The Value of the Podcast

In the era Nicholas Quah calls 'Big Podcasting', the dust of the Wild West has settled and the roads are being paved with gold as Spotify, Luminary, Audible and BBC Sounds march ever onward, scooping up the sexiest talent and ramping up the playing field to a whole new level.

Independent production companies, ravenous for commissions, devour just about any millennial who can talk about politics and contouring in the same sentence, like Pacmen in a field of tall poppies.

Awards

The term 'preferred suppliers', that elite list of production companies which are allowed into the hallowed gates of BBC radio, is back. For those who love the punk spirit of DIY podcasting in which a duvet over the head often provides the only 'studio' many podcasters will ever need, this has changed the game. While the big players with their teams of editors and technicians can bring quality and therefore bigger audiences to the playing field, it kicks the ball out of the park for the vast majority of podcasters. And most don't seem to give a damn. Podcasting is all about playing your own game.

We've read – and you can hear on *How to Grow a Pod* – of George the Poet's success prior to his patronage by BBC Sounds and he has nothing but good things to say about his new partners. 'They didn't touch a thing,' he told me. BBC Sounds doesn't just mean access to technical excellence but the use of music which will transform any audio storytelling into a thing of beauty.

Looking through the list of winners in the various categories of the 2019 British Podcast Awards, it's clear that podcasting is not what it was. BBC Sounds' *Brexitcast*, BBC 5 Live's *You, Me and the Big C*, BBC's *The Grenfell Tower Inquiry with Eddie Mair*, BBC 5 Live's *Surrogacy: A Family Frontier*, 5 Live's *That Peter Crouch Podcast*, BBC Sounds' *Multi Story*, Classic FM's *Case Notes* ... British Podcasting is being colonised by British Broadcasting.

It's a no-brainer. When the *delicious.* podcast was nominated at the Fortnum and Mason Awards in 2017 for Best Radio or Podcast Award, it was up against Radio 4's flagship series, the legendary *Food Programme*, which has almost single-handedly put the politics of food into the British public consciousness for forty years. The other nominees included a BBC Belfast food programme and *The Kitchen Cabinet*, produced by preferred supplier Somethin' Else for Radio 4 and presented by award-winning food writer and food critic at the *Observer*, Jay Rayner. It was lovely to be invited to the party, but of course the plucky little *delicious.* podcast, researched, produced, edited and voiced by me on a budget of next to nothing and recorded under a duvet, could never win.

Podcast pioneer Suzy Buttress of *The Casual Birder* podcast says she feels a little jaded. 'I tried early on to go for the British Podcast Awards,' she told me. 'I believed in my show. I didn't get anywhere and that was quite a knockback.' She says she was 'lucky enough' to go to the awards with a friend who won a bronze. 'I was so happy to support her there and it was really lovely to go along and see what goes on at the awards. But I know it's not for me. I don't think I would ever put myself forward for an award again. I think for my show, I'm happy with the feedback I get from my listeners – and I get feedback from the same people week after week so I know they're listening.'

The cost of quality

Matt Hill is one of the founders of the BPAs. His *Guardian* food podcast

Let's Eat was a nominee for the Best Radio or Podcast Award at the 2018 Fortnum and Mason Awards. I asked him what, without the quality that time, money, a studio and an editorial team can give a podcast, awards could possibly offer the vast majority of podcasters. He told me that this is a constant question behind the scenes at the BPAs. 'We think a lot about what makes a good podcast,' he tells me, 'and should sound quality be a mitigating factor? Or whether it should be focused on the content.'

His answer is a bit fluffy. 'I think, essentially, as long as the focus was deliberate, what the producers or the presenter wanted you to focus in on was the thing that you could hear the most, then it didn't matter. What you didn't want was it to be distorted or hard to hear, because that would mean that you weren't hitting your audience, for very valid reasons: people have very low tolerance for bad audio.'

In the true spirit of DIY podcasting, Matt insists that you don't need to spend money on a studio to get good sound. 'I predominately record outside of studios, and the overriding factor for me is more one of convenience. Like, could we get this person into a studio? No. Well then, let's go to their house. Let's go to their office, let's turn their office into a makeshift studio.' *The Week Unwrapped* with Olly Mann is recorded in 'one of those terrible glass meeting rooms on the top floor' of *The Week*'s building. But Matt insists that it is covered in foam once a week for the team, which he says cost them 'like £60 three years ago, and we're still using all that kit. So, I don't think it's about affordability. It looks terrible but sounds pretty good. And I think that's the important thing.'

He disagrees that the BBC scoops up the majority of big wins at the BPAs and gives me a sneak peek at the nominations for 2020. 'The BBC haven't won anywhere near 50 per cent of the nominations because there's a really healthy independent sector now. And, of course, other larger broadcasters are getting involved. But actually, independents are still the majority of nominees. And last year, the big winner [George the Poet's and Benbrick's *Have You Heard George's Podcast?*] had fewer than 5,000 listeners before they came to the awards.'

Sponsors

The healthy independent sector he refers to is growing rapidly, offering jobs in podcasting, trying out stories for TV or film, building audiences for podcasts across the board and bringing money to the party, and it seems that everyone wants a slice of the cake. Sponsors can come in all shapes and sizes, and in a world in which everyone is making it up as they go along, Matt Hill suggests that you give a sponsor the opportunity to turn you down. You might be happily surprised. 'I suppose it depends on what you go into making your podcast for. If it's for money, it's getting more difficult in the sense that there are lots of other big beasts in that pool.' But he says that those 'big beasts' have demanded a lot more attention. 'So, not only have you got the Apple podcast spot front page, now you've got Spotify creating playlists, you've got PR companies set up primarily to plug podcasts in various broadsheets and tabloids. You've got the British Podcast Awards now. I mean, there are so many more outlets because the money has come into the industry and there are opportunities there. I'm not saying they're necessarily equal opportunities, but they are there for the taking. If you're hungry enough you can at least get into some of those places. Both Apple and Spotify have human beings curating their front pages. There's no reason why you can't push at that door.'

But if you *can* persuade a sponsor to support you, you do have a lot to offer. Podcast listeners are often more devoted and responsive than audiences in other mediums and are therefore valuable to the right sponsor. Even a small audience can bring results. The going rate, if there is such a thing, is $20–$30 per thousand downloads per episode, measured four to six weeks after release, but Matt Hill suggests thinking laterally. 'What we try and do is look at what the pricing structure is for different media, and just port them over to podcasting. So, if you're doing a trade podcast for a very specific group of people, or a horse racing podcast, then you might look at your listenership of, say, 6000 people, call up the *Racing Post* desk and ask them how much a quarter-page ad in their magazine is. And that could be your mid-roll ad price. You have value in your listeners, particularly that small scale. If you've got a very targeted, focused group that you know are the only ones that could possibly be listening, who love horse racing above other things, that's the kind of audience that has a value and you should charge on that basis.'

He suggests charging a full-page ad rate for a pre-roll sponsor read at the front of the podcast episode which has more cachet, even though, as he says, it's the easiest bit to skip!

Lateral thinking

But it's coming up with the fun ways to make money that will appeal to most podcasters. 'I think it is really important to think about the low-hanging fruit,' he said, looking at where the value of a podcast can be hiding. 'Who do you have access to on your mailing lists, among your subscribers, your other media, your brand? Where is that audience?' Understanding that might lead to the confidence to negotiate a contra deal with a sponsor purely to build your audience and give your new podcast greater value. It could be a free-of-charge sponsor read in exchange for a call to action to sign up for your mailing list, for example. Thinking laterally is in the DNA of podcasting culture.

Matt has given me an idea. *Cooking the Books* is a niche and new podcast which according to Buzzsprout's calculations (p.69) reaches well into the top 7 per cent of global thirty-day downloads. Its listeners are food lovers and they love to hear their favourite A-lister food writers talk to me about food. That must have value to a food producer, retailer or anyone who wants to specifically target food fans. But it takes so much time to find a suitable sponsor by myself, and time is money. So what about if I upped the offer? What if I could find a company to join me in pioneering a new way of bringing brands to podcasts? In return for lending my podcast their social media clout over a period of time, I would give them a series of sponsor reads, a free-of-charge sponsorship deal that served us both. Telling my listeners about their campaign or product in return for a series of swipe-up-to-listens on Instagram could grow my audience to something that really would have value. And quickly.

And so, I did. In return for weaving four sponsor reads about Whole Foods' Mindful Moments guide to organic and responsibly sourced products each week, Whole Foods Market posted weekly swipe-up-to-listen promotions on Instagram stories for a month, offering its 199,000 followers a direct link to *Cooking the Books*. It was a win-win.

And in the podcasting world of smoke and mirrors, perception adds value. Colleagues began to email: 'Hey, well done on getting Whole Foods as a sponsor,' wrote one. Publicists began to spot an opportunity to place their clients in front of my audience. Louisa Ham of Stella PR was already looking for ways to help her client, super-sustainable organic chocolate Montezuma, tell the stories behind their brand. The homemade chocolate's husband-and-wife owners wanted to talk about their commitment to 'substance over style . . . and sustainable and organic business growth over greed'. Louisa heard the Whole Foods sponsor reads, knew that *Cooking the Books* reflected my own delicious sustainability agenda and arranged for a month of sponsorship. As a result, more publicists are getting in touch. 'I've just been listening to the episode with Yottam and Ixta and Montezuma really do get a fantastic plug at the beginning there!', wrote one of them. 'I've passed on these details to the rest of the team and we will absolutely bear in mind as we plan for 2021.' Success clearly breeds success.

POD POINTS

- What's the real value of your podcast?
- It's not always about the awards!
- What can a sponsor offer your podcast other than just cash?

20

The Network 3.0

The phrase 'Better together' might remind you of the tension around Scotland's 2011 pro-union campaign, but in Podcastland it's not a bad shout. As we know, most podcasters are hobbyists, squirrelling themselves away after the day job to indulge their passion project. The lesser-spotted podcaster with headphone hair and tiny pupils after hours of staring at a ProTools edit is a solitary creature, but even for those who love nothing more than a dark room and a world through sound, there's a secret longing to be part of a tribe. Enter: The network.

Community of practice

Principally the point of a network is to create a shared revenue between a number of podcasts. For advertisers looking for a way to test the waters in podcasting, placing an ad with a network which hosts hundreds of podcasts with big audiences is an easy option. With most podcasters averaging between 130 and 145 downloads per episode, there's an argument for doing it yourself. After all, isn't that the point of podcasting? A community of practice can be anything from a bunch of film podcasters to food fans who love to explore every aspect of their subject, but although this is a growing area of podcasting, advertisers buy their space based on CPM (cost per thousand listeners) and most networks are looking for shows that average 50,000 downloads per month.

Listener support

Helen Zaltzman's *The Allusionist* is part of podcasting supergroup Radiotopia, a network of cutting-edge shows curated by Roman Mars which include his own consistently chart-topping *99% Invisible*. Creators are better together in Radiotopia, particularly if you're not the kind of person who likes to ask for money. 'It's still listener-supported,' said Helen. 'We have annual funding drives and there's usually some kind of rewards they can have, but most of them just want to translate their emotions into money. I was very uncomfortable asking them to do that the first time, because I was like, well, no one's making me make a free podcast, but they want to do that.' And the giver's gain works; she's now supporting the next generation of podcasters. 'Now that I have some money, which I didn't for the first eight years of podcasting, I like redistributing it to other podcasts. It's supporting what they make and knowing that all the money's going into the production rather than a big office building and layers of commissioners and people getting in the way of the creator. The system I'm in is that if listeners give me money, it goes directly to make more of the thing that they like. And I think they like that.'

Helen is one of the increasing number of patrons who promotes direct support for content creators in terms of donations. She says that it's a more active way of supporting your favourite podcasters. 'If you're listening to something like Spotify and you're paying the subscription fee, you might think that you've done your bit, but you haven't. None of the podcasters you listen to on Spotify are getting that money. The only podcasts making money on Spotify are the ones that Spotify has bought or funded with that capital.'

But it takes a tech-savvy podcaster to manage their own online payments and those who do ask for 'beer money' will turn to companies like PayPal and Patreon for help. Patreon encourages creators to run a subscription content service for their followers by providing exclusive rewards and perks to their subscribers. The transaction is clearer: your patrons pay you and in return, you create special content for them as well as your usual output, although several Patreon creators I spoke to quietly admitted to feeling the pressure to perform for often little return.

It's not (just) about the money

Matt Hill thinks that it's fine to go into podcasting with ambition, but the ambition primarily should be to make a good show. 'It should be the best version of itself and doing something for the listener. And if you do that, then there's the possibility of making money as well.' He thinks, as I do, that success is about making something that is so much more than cash. 'It doesn't have to be a big success,' he said, 'it just has to be right for those people at that time.' He thinks that a podcaster needs to have a very simple mindset: 'We've got to think, *What is the reasonable size of this audience, and what is the amount of time we're willing to put in to make it?* And then, sometimes, the sponsorship might cover that. And if it doesn't, are there other revenue streams? And if there aren't, is it worth being made? Sometimes it is, just for the love.'

Enter the entrepreneurs

But where there's an audience, however small, there's usually an entrepreneur sizing up the gap in the market. Enter Podimo, a new Danish open podcast platform which throws its hat in the podcasting ring with a UK launch in 2021 promising a revenue share model driven by a subscription-based service.

It's already going great guns in Denmark, Germany and Spain with plans to focus on podcasters of all levels. 'Whether you're putting your first podcast out in the world or already hitting the charts, we want to show podcasters that you can have a slice of the pie,' Sophie Paluch from the UK team told me. 'I think a lot of existing platforms make many podcasters feel like unless they are a top-twenty podcast, the chances of making any money are quite slim. A lot of podcasters I've spoken to think the big brand sponsorship and advertising deals are for the big names and big pods. We want to create a different way for them to generate revenue that isn't so reliant on that model.'

It's all about the 'ecosystem', according to CEO and founder Morten Strunge. The idea is to bring more listeners through a platform curated by a combination of machine power and real people, hot from their experiences on the teams of Spotify, Netflix and YouTube, that gives a wider variety of good podcasts the chance to be discovered.

Podcasters swapping their existing host to join Podimo will be able to choose between being exclusively listed on Podimo in return for a 50 per cent share of the revenue or continue to be listed on Apple, Spotify and all the usual directories (p.88) and still receive 20 per cent. For the listener, the monthly subscription fee is split only among the podcasts they have listened to that month, giving them a new way to support their heroes. 'If you're out there making great content and growing your audience then you should be able to earn and be rewarded for that so you can keep on doing it,' said Sophie.

It does make sense. Remember what Jason Allan Scott told us about 'podfade'? The average podcaster makes between three and five episodes before giving up. Podfade may be the universe's way of sorting the wheat from the chaff, but for many podcasters with good shows and engaged audiences, raising sponsorship or courting advertisers is a skill too far and justifying time spent on a zero-return pod can become tricky. Maybe if, as Helen Zaltzman said earlier, Spotify's subscription revenue barely ever reaches the podcast creators, there's room for a new name in town.

But podcasters in Helen's Facebook Podcasters' Support Group were not quite so convinced. Colin Jackson-Brown, from *Free With This Month's Issue* podcast, responded to my post about this new subscription-based service. 'I really don't like this move towards certain podcasts only being available on certain platforms,' he wrote, 'particularly ones that are behind a paywall. To me it's the antithesis of what podcasting should be. I don't want it to become the norm that podcast listeners have to have multiple subscriptions to different platforms to listen to all the shows they like in the same way as having Netflix, Disney+, Nowtv, etc. I stopped listening to *The Last Podcast On The Left* on principle when they went Spotify exclusive even though I have a Spotify subscription.'

Helen Zaltzman was also unimpressed: 'Unless you're available exclusively to a huge platform (so just Spotify and Apple, realistically),' she posted, 'you're not going to have much audience nor, therefore, much revenue. You have a much better chance of making more money the more places your show is available (again, except in the rare cases Spotify pays you a shitload for exclusivity).' But, like me, Niall Killeney-Taylor of the *Corona Diaries* podcast had spoken directly to the Podimo UK team and was similarly excited. 'The company ethos,' he wrote, 'is very much about working with the creators and making sure there is a fair share in revenue, unlike many others. Also, I don't think it has to be exclusive only to Podimo. I believe if it is a Podimo original then it would be exclusive to the network for a short period before being available across all platforms. Seeing what is going on with a lot of other networks at the moment, they seem to be one that genuinely is trying to do well by the creators.'

Perhaps the biggest problem that Podimo faces is one that online newspapers have been grappling with for years. If you've always had your listening for free, why would you start paying for it? A curated experience which pays your heroes might be worth supporting, and only time will tell just how loyal podfans really are.

POD POINTS

- A network can add clout to your profile
- Fans *want* to support you. Give them a way to do so
- The market is changing fast and giving listeners and podcasters new opportunities to pay and get paid

Conclusion: Forecast

We're well into what's become known as the Big Era of podcasting as Spotify continues to roll its tanks into town, acquiring people and production companies and counting the cash along the way. Luminary may have failed in its bid to gild its lilies as it hoiked huge stars like Russell Brand behind its paywall, losing friends and influence as it did so, but succeeding in its initial plan to become the Netflix of podcasting, luring us into its subscription service with a tantalising selection of ad-free shows, is surely an inevitability.

In July 2020, satellite radio channel SiriusXM bought Stitcher, the premium ad-free subscription podcasting app which podwatchers believe will raise the stakes in the race for dominance of the podcasting space currently being won by Spotify, iHeartMedia and Apple. We've seen how celebrity podcasts have brought millions of new listeners to the platform and with them rich new seams of sponsorship and advertising.

But in the chasm that divides the boardrooms and the bedrooms a new space is beginning to settle which looks rather promising. Not so long ago, audio production companies made programmes for the few BBC radio stations that commission independent shows but are now sharing their table-football breaks with ad men and women as brands train their teams to sit in at the research stage. A whole new raft of audio producers and presenters are coming out of their bedrooms with passion podcasts on their CVs and a social media following that's creating conversations and an evolution if not a revolution in the audio industry.

Helen Zaltzman regularly uses the Facebook Podcasters' Support Group to post job opportunities that she spots, but is sceptical about the role of a podcaster in big media organisations. 'The creator always seems to lose out first,' she told me. 'The big money years have not resulted in more creators getting more opportunities or more money. It's turned them into employees – *low-power* employees. And I find that very disagreeable and frustrating.'

Hana Walker-Brown, executive producer at Broccoli, the London-based podcast production company that was founded to counter the lack of opportunities for minority talent both in front of and behind the mic, says that it doesn't have to be that way. 'There's a crazy amount of money going into podcasting now. There's over a million podcasts on Apple right now,' she said. 'And I would say probably only a small percentage are making money. But in America, this industry is absolutely booming. There's more money in podcasting than there is in TV. A lot of the time podcasts are being turned into TV. Now they're doing it the other way around. They're like, "What can we make into a podcast?"' She predicts that the same will happen in the UK, opening up a new audio industry which will attract 'exceptionally talented people from all over podcasting, not just production and presenting, but [those in] marketing strategy'.

Broccoli, whose tag line is 'content that's good for you', has taken the American model and given it a healthy diversity spin, with a strong commitment to creating real change in the media industry. It is the first podcasting production joint venture launched outside the US by Sony Music Entertainment, and could be part of the future of podcasting. It was founded by Renay Richardson, the first content manager at Acast's London office and part of the acquisition team behind the platform's biggest shows including Scroobius Pip's *Distraction Pieces Podcast* and *The Adam Buxton Podcast*, and who, as an independent producer, was part of the success of the award-winning podcast *The Receipts* on BBC1xtra in 2018.

Richardson created the Equality in Audio Pact in 2020 which pledges to take action towards equality. The pact promises to pay interns; hire LGBTQIA+, black people, people of colour and other minorities on projects not only related to their identity; to release race pay gap data along with gender pay gap reports; to avoid panels that are not representative of the cities, towns and industries they take place in and to be transparent about who works for your company as well as their role, position and permanency. Josh Adley at Listen says that it's a step in the right direction. 'The BBC have signed up, along with 250 production companies and podcasts,' he told me. 'It's really got a lot of attention in our industry and brought the issue to the front of mind.'

Hana believes that it could be a game-changer as the industry produces more of the kind of top-level podcasts made by Ira Glass and Gimlet Media; 'the ones,' said Hana, 'with a hundred million downloads which have had an elite team behind them. *Serial* didn't just pop out of nowhere; it's years and years of work and graft by journalists presenting and scripting. The team is exceptional.'

Her series *Anthems* for Broccoli is an example of how the pact works creatively. It was initially conceived as a response to Hana's frustration about the lack of feminist podcasting other than around International Women's Day on 8 March every year. She had already made *To the Woman* for Audible, a clarion call of twenty women's voices aching to be heard. At Broccoli, Hana wondered how to expand on it. 'There are *so* many women's voices,' she told me, 'and [yet] I've been in meetings where powerful women have said that they can't for the life of them think of a good female presenter. I've been flabbergasted. And you wonder why we aren't progressing.'

Hana's first series for Broccoli was inspired partly by the division she had witnessed between women on the subject of their own equal rights. 'I'd had conversations with friends who have all the kind of morals and traits and ethos of being feminists, but they won't use the word. They're like, "But I'm not like her, or I'm not like her."' A podcast series would allow for nuance, the depth to explore feminism itself but through personal experiences. Hana felt that two kinds of feminists were emerging: 'There were the old-school feminists, but then there was the very young, middle-class, mostly white, affluent feminist, probably with parents who were either successful or didn't have to work. It excludes so many people.'

She felt the need to do something ambitious, to explore what it means to be a woman. She pitched her idea to Broccoli. 'Let's release a show every single day,' she told Renay and the team. 'I'll sound design every single one and we'll get thirty-one women to write pieces on what it means to be a woman.' It would become the first series of *Anthems,* the ten-minute pieces that tell how life is for people who are not usually given a platform. 'We needed new kinds of rallying cries. We needed new words that we could sing out to each other. We needed new manifestos.'

It was a powerful piece of podcasting history. 'It was short,' said Hana. 'People were really into that after a ten-episode true crime drama every day.' Broccoli commissioned another series, this time to celebrate Pride with a daily essay from voices rarely heard outside their communities. 'It's both a call to arms and a celebration,' said Hana. 'A party and protest. Pride was such a great fit because that's how Pride was born.' The series is now feeding itself. 'When lockdown hit, we thought, *What can we do for those who have lost all their work and all their money that might want to do something creative?*' With Black History Month providing a wealth of material for *Anthems,* there's a lot of work to do and a vibrant team of podcasters finding value and a career in what they have to say. 'Everybody gets paid,' said Hana. 'no one's doing anything for free. Nothing is like a favour.'

It's a wonderful vision of how the punk philosophy of podcasting has changed the sound of protest. But without the might of Sony

Music investing in them, I wonder how this leap in media history helps the hobbyist. Hana told me that she thinks that the gap will close. 'Especially after a lockdown situation where audio has been thriving, it's something people can do safely, securely and professionally. I think that middle ground exists. Look at *The Receipts* [*Podcast*] girls, they're doing absolutely incredibly. They have the most insane following and they didn't even know each other before they started this. It's just testament to great content and what people need.'

For millions of podcasters who care less about the quality of their sound than gathering a following of like-minded hobbyists, their content may not be what an award-winning sound producer like Hana might call 'great'. And that's the glory of podcasting. It's a platform that gives a voice to anyone who has something to say. It just might not pay the rent. It's a free-for-all with a low entry level and, very often, a good return on investment – if only in love, respect and community for the huge majority. And for those with an entrepreneurial bent it's an extraordinary opportunity to do it yourself and reap the rewards, leveraging yourself to wherever you want to be. I fancied hosting a stage at the World of Words at WOMAD and so I did, chairing a panel discussion on veganism in a tent full of food activists and frustrated farmers. I lusted over sharing the bill on the podcast stage at Latitude with Cariad Lloyd of *Griefcast*, Mark Kermode, Tracey McLeod and Marcus Brigstocke, and so I did, even if a bad back meant that I couldn't make it on the day. And I was invited to write the first book to celebrate the warm and fuzzy world of podcasting. Who knows where my podcasting adventures will lead me?

But for most of the hobbyists podcasting will continue to be a gift to their listeners, uncompromised by grubby old money. We've met many of them in the chapters of this book, the birdwatchers, the folk singers, the gay history archivists who just want to talk to people who share their interests. They don't covet the stage shows or the book deals, the Netflix contract or the auction that sells their passion project to the highest bidder. The endless fascination with celebrities, the human desire to worship them as gods, doesn't cut the mustard in the quiet lanes of Podcastland where millions of niche podcasters are chatting happily to their tribes.

They are the ones who have created communities and engaged listeners in a way that has never happened before, but will they see the spoils, and do they care? I asked the Podcasters' Support Group, who cover the entire range from passion projecters to serious pros, for their prediction or wish for the future of podcasting. Márcio Barcelos of *Sobretudo* podcast said that his prediction was not his wish: 'Fortified castles surrounded by paywalls which you'll need to subscribe to [in order] to listen, like you do with cable TV and streaming services today.' Lisa Francesca Nand of *The Big Travel Podcast* wrote: 'Podcasts are going to continue their trajectory to become even more mainstream and interchangeable with radio listening as we have seen with TV versus watching on demand.' 'Podcasts are going to be a respected form of media and one that teachers will use as an adjunct to other materials,' wrote Elizabeth Macduffie of *Dystopian States of America* podcast. Rashmi Patel of *Living to Love Ourself* podcast wrote: 'My wish is to expand awareness and educate health through the power of our voice.' Tony from Pennsylvania, USA, commented: 'Not far into the future ... a mega company will rename "podcasts" to something everyone will understand, and suddenly "Internet Talk Shows" will take off to new heights! "IT'S the future! You heard it here first!"

Meanwhile, in the leafy lanes and top-floor flats of Podcastland, podjocks are donning their headphones and clicking into their Zoom rooms to spend another evening chatting to their heroes and counting the beer money from their fans. The *My Dad Wrote a Porno* team are on Instagram to announce the cancellation of their 2020 tour and *Table Manners* is posting recipes from its cookbook. I check into the online forums. 'Can I get away with one "twat" without marking it explicit?' asks a podcaster, and a lunchtime thread begins to ping with a mix of legal advice and banter. It's a hobbyist world with a punk ethos that for all the chat about celebrity domination and #sizematters is unlikely to change, and I can't think of a single reason why I won't be making podcasts for the rest of my life.

As I write, the Podcast Movement forum is busily answering an existential question from a podcaster: Why do you podcast? The answers tell the story of a community from across the world who have everything and nothing in common:

- Because I got a lot of stuff to say LOL.
- Because I enjoy storytelling and wanted to give normal people a chance to tell their story.
- To change the old-fashioned narratives for women in midlife and beyond.
- I failed at getting a book published.
- To make big bucks doing very little work.
- To have my own project to work on as opposed to constantly investing my interest and skillset in my job.
- To connect with like-minded people and share my perspective and thoughts.
- Tell my stories my way!
- Because I am a narcissist that loves the sound of her own voice.

Acknowledgements

Thanks to the thousands of podcasters who share this make-it-up, have-a-go world of passion projects and professional pods, whose trials and errors punctuate my days with a quick pop into the forums. I love their honesty and bluff, their endlessly helpful ideas and genuinely inspiring stories. They are the heartbeat of podcasting and a community that has made Podcastland the most desirable of destinations, even if its roads are not always paved with gold. Thanks to those who shared their stories in this book, in particular the *Casual Birder* podcaster, Suzy Buttress, Jon Wilks of *Old Songs* and James Ramsden of *The Kitchen is on Fire*.

Thanks to the podcasting pioneers who filled this book with their wit and wisdom: Helen Zaltzman, podcasting matriarch and Miss Whiplash of the Facebook Podcasters' Support Group, where you'll find me leaning on the bar most lunchtimes; her co-host of *Answer Me This!* and poly-podder, Olly Mann; British Podcast Awards' Matt Hill; A-lister podcats Alice Levine, Jamie Morton and James Cooper from *My Dad Wrote a Porno*; Jessie and Lennie Ware; George the Poet; and, of course, *This American Life* legend Ira Glass.

Thanks to pioneering podcast producers Georgia Catt of *The Missing Cryptoqueen*, Karen Rose, Alison Vernon-Smith, Chris Hogg, Hana Walker-Brown and the business brains pumping up the podcast's potential: Jason Allan Scott, Josh Adley, Danny Lowney, Daniel Levine and Cressida Ward of Food Tryb and Sophie Paluch of Podimo.

ACKNOWLEDGEMENTS

Thanks to would-be podcasters Peta Wilkinson and Adam Reeves and my husband, Jed Novick, for reading through the draft manuscript. And to my editor, Tom Asker at Robinson, for giving me the kind of notes and feedback that every author craves. Huge thanks to fellow Robinson writer Sam Gates for the introduction to Tom while she was on my podcasting retreat, and to my agent Charlie Brotherstone.

Afterword

As a person who runs a podcast production company, the question I get asked the most is: 'Is there money in podcasting?' The simple answer is: Yes, and there is enough to go around. But that does not mean it will go around, and I believe this is why that question is asked so frequently.

Before I began working in the audio industry, I had spent the previous fifteen years working in film and television. I began as a child actor before working my way up the ladder at a talent agency from the mailroom. After nine years in talent management, I moved on to working at a television production company and finally ended the run on film and television sets working in the production offices. Recently, I was reminded that I have carried over a lot of knowledge from those past roles and one of the main things I learned very early on is that around 99 per cent of actors are unemployed. That isn't to say that 99 per cent of actors are not currently working; this just means they are not employed as actors. This is something that has stayed with me my whole career and I think about it a lot. When I am asked whether there is money in podcasting, this is often how I answer, because it is relevant to nearly all creative industries. There is money, but just like most industries, only 1 per cent prosper.

The podcast industry is changing, and it is changing fast with big players making major moves, showing that they are backing podcasting as the next big creative growth market. Companies known for music like Spotify and Sony Music are making heavy investments in podcasting, while Apple are working to change the perception that they are just a podcast app in the market. But what does this mean for the little guy? It means he needs to diversify, but I think the industry always called for that.

I am one of the rare audio producers in the UK who has not worked at the BBC. My first audio job was at Acast in 2014 as the UK Content Manager. Very early on I fell in love with podcasting and the opportunities the medium grants creators. It was and still is one of the only mediums where you can be completely independent and disconnected from the wider industry and succeed. You can ignore the rules of what went before you; you can experiment; you can be any age, any race, any gender and any ability. In podcasting none of these things matter; you can go and create your own show and put it out into the world.

But you have to diversify if you want to succeed. By this I mean you cannot be just one thing. You cannot just host a podcast, or just produce a podcast, or just market, consult or strategise. You have to acquire skills in every aspect of podcasting. I'm not saying you have to be an expert, but you do need knowledge of what happens in every aspect of podcasting.

I worked as a content manager at Acast, a production coordinator at Audible and as a producer at Panoply before going it alone into freelancing and then founding my company Broccoli Content. Even before I started any of these audio industry jobs I had acquired transferable skills in my earlier film and television career, and I recognised early on that diversifying was important. If you host a show, can you produce someone else's? Can you consult on business or marketing strategy? Can you be a people person so that you can network and build meaningful relationships? I will never claim to be excellent or an expert in any of these things, but I do recognise that they are important and that anyone who is in podcasting or who wants to be can navigate the industry successfully if they keep this in mind.

As I look to the future of podcasting and what may happen, it is hard to predict because we are still so early on in its inception. Technology and priorities change at breakneck speed and they dictate the route podcasting will take. Having worked in television, I can see how similar that industry is to podcasting, and I feel fairly confident that these two creative juggernauts will continue to be linked, with the pipeline of podcast-to-TV and TV-to-podcast projects happening more and more.

Personally, one thing I hope for is that companies and creators begin to see the benefits of diversifying their guests and who they work with. This will not only lead to more opportunities for people in the industry but also gives us all the chance to grow our listenership. I do believe one day you will be able to travel anywhere in the world and ask any person what their favourite podcast is – just like you can with books, music and film – and they will have an answer.

Big corporations will continue to enter the podcasting space with consolidations set to rise. I hope this doesn't push the smaller shows to the side and instead leads to more collaboration and experimentation. Podcasting is going to become more and more competitive which means it will be slightly harder to make a mark but still not impossible. With competition comes growth and in the long term a healthier industry will bring a multitude of opportunity. The future of podcasting may seem daunting but just keep in mind with change comes opportunity. There has never been a better time to start a podcast, if you have the ideas, get recording and find your audience. Podcasting is for everyone.

Renay Richardson, founder and CEO, Broccoli Content